Keeping Cats

By now I had my eyes shut so I couldn't see how dark it was. My heart was beating so loud that I couldn't hear anything else.

Sophie discovers that Mr Wetherall is going to drown a whole family of kittens, but no one will listen to her. So she sneaks down to the canal, in the night, to rescue them . . .

But that's only the start of the problems. How do you hide five noisy, hungry kittens from everyone— even your own family? And what do you do when you are found out? Sophie tells her own story in this funny, moving book.

Jay Ashton was brought up in London, and worked in various places including Uganda and France, before settling in South Wales which she loved and where she lived and wrote. She was fascinated by nature, was actively involved in wildlife conservation, and was always surrounded by animals. Sadly, Jay died recently. She leaves one son.

Keeping Cats

Other books by Jay Ashton

Looking for Ilyriand
The Door from Nowhere
Killing the Demons

Keeping Cats

or

Picking Up the Litter

Jay Ashton

Oxford University Press
Oxford New York Toronto

Oxford University Press, Great Clarendon Street,
Oxford OX2 6DP

Oxford New York
Athens Auckland Bangkok Bogota Bombay
Buenos Aires Calcutta Cape Town Dar es Salaam
Delhi Florence Hong Kong Istanbul Karachi
Kuala Lumpur Madras Madrid Melbourne
Mexico City Nairobi Paris Singapore
Taipei Tokyo Toronto

and associated companies in
Berlin Ibadan

Oxford is a trade mark of Oxford University Press

Cover illustration by Patricia Moffett
Cover design by Slatter-Anderson

A CIP catalogue record for this book is available
from the British Library

ISBN 0 19 271581 X

Printed and bound in Great Britain by
Biddles Ltd, Guildford and King's Lynn

This book is dedicated to Oliver (and Hardy, his tail) who started it all, and to the rest of the team: Hazel (Top Cat), Holly (Office Manager), Barnaby Ashton-Boing (Deputy Dog) and Ceri (Public Relations).

My name is Sophie Marriott. At least, that was my name at the beginning of this story. When I leave school I'm going to be famous. That's why I'm writing this, because when I'm famous everyone will want to know how it all started.

PART ONE

CHAPTER ONE

'Do you want to see my kittens?' asked Tracy on the way home from school.

'Don't mind,' I said. If I showed any enthusiasm Tracy would turn round and say she wouldn't let me see them.

'Come on, then,' said Tracy severely. 'Don't dawdle.'

I did my best to keep up with Tracy's long legs. We weren't really friends, but we lived close and Tracy's friend was away sick. I usually went home on my own.

Tracy was way ahead, turning into her street. 'Come *on*, Sophie,' she yelled. 'You're too slow to catch a cold.'

Right then I felt I was more likely to go down with heatstroke. The road ran uphill, and I was panting. Heat bounced up off the concrete. The doors of the terraced houses opened straight on to the pavement, and there were no trees, only parked cars and toddlers on trundle toys.

'We'll go round the back,' said Tracy. 'I got the back door key.'

She led the way down a narrow alley between the houses and out into a burst of sunshine and green leaves. To make up for the lack of front gardens, the back gardens were long and stretched down to the canal. On the far side were allotments and more gardens before the next row of houses. I wanted to stop and look. It was like discovering a secret world. Tracy didn't seem to notice.

'Good raspberries in here,' she said, leaning over a ramshackle fence to pick the swollen fruit.

I was expecting someone to start shouting. 'Whose are they?' I asked.

Tracy was all over juice. 'Old lady lives there. Never goes into her garden. Look at the state of it. My dad's always grumbling about the weeds, says they blow over on to ours.' She opened the gate of the next garden, neat, not a leaf out of place. There were rows of runner beans splashed with scarlet flowers, and big-headed cabbages, and some pointy things.

Tracy saw me looking at them. 'Asparagus,' she said in a show-off sort of voice. 'Dad wins prizes with his asparagus.'

'Oh.' My dad has to be persuaded even to mow the lawn.

Tracy unlocked the back door. 'They're in here,' she said, pointing to a tea-chest in a corner of the kitchen.

At first I could make out nothing but a vague black heap. Then a pair of green eyes gleamed and the mother stood up. She stretched front legs, then back legs, then seemed to flow out of the chest and disappeared through the back door. The heap stirred, showing bits of ears, some tails, blue eyes, and one pink tongue. I couldn't work out what belonged to which or how many there were.

'Five. Here.' Tracy pulled out a kitten and passed it over.

I still couldn't see it properly: it nestled under my neck, warm and a bit smelly and bit my ear. 'What's its name?' I asked, trying to arrange it properly and getting scratched.

'Oh, I call them all Kitty,' said Tracy, hitching herself up on to the worktop. 'I can't tell them apart so one name does for all of them. Flaming fleas,' she went on, scratching her leg. The kitten I was holding jumped down so I lifted the others out of the chest. Tracy wasn't taking any notice, was busy scratching her right buttock.

The kittens spread out looking like animated blobs of the stuff that comes out of vacuum-cleaner bags. They had two pointy bits at the front for ears and another pointy bit at the back for a tail. And they did all look the same. I could see what Tracy meant, but still it seemed a bit heartless to make them all share a name.

One of them was stalking another, oozing along on its tummy, eyes intent, whiskers quivering. Suddenly, it pounced on its quarry and the two rolled over, kicking. They were behaving just like the lions on *Wildlife on One* the other night, except at that size it was ridiculous.

I caught one and it snuggled up, rubbing its cheek against my hand, and purred. I asked Tracy how old they were.

'Six weeks nearly,' said Tracy. 'They've got to go tonight.'

'You've found homes for them?' I asked, thinking, *rats*. I'd been working out how to persuade Mum and Dad they needed a kitten.

'Oh no. Dad'll drown them.'

'Drown them?' I thought I must have misheard.

'Of course. Soon as they're six weeks. When their mum stops feeding them they cost too much.'

'But *drown* them?'

Tracy shrugged. 'Nobody wants them. And there's the canal at the bottom of the garden.' She shrieked as a kitten tried to haul itself up her bare leg. 'Little pest,' she said fondly, prising it off and dropping it back in the chest.

I ran all the way home from Tracy's house. I needn't have bothered, though: my parents weren't back from work. As usual. Instead there was the sound of my brother's guitar from upstairs and Rug sitting on the doormat waiting to be let in. He had a cat flap in the back door but it was ages since he had been able to get through that without a struggle. As I opened the door he got up—he had so much fur you couldn't see his legs—and surged in. I fed him, then poured two glasses of Coke and went upstairs. It would be useful to have an ally.

'If you're going to Scarborough Fair,' my brother was singing as I went along the landing, 'Parsley, sage, rosemary, and thyme—' He stopped as I went into his room.

'I brought you a drink,' I said, with my best charming smile. We hated each other's guts really.

'What do you want? I'm busy.'

'Zack . . .' I sat on the end of his bed, next to the tank of piranhas. My brother's name is Richard but he's going to be a folk singer and if you want anything out of him you have to call him Zack. 'There's these kittens,' I said. 'They'll be drowned if we don't save them.'

He swallowed the Coke in one and burped. 'We've got a cat,' he pointed out.

That was irrelevant, so I ignored it. 'There's five of them and Tracy's dad is going to put them in a sack and throw them in the canal.' Just saying it made me feel sick.

'Stop that,' said Zack.

'What? . . . Oh.' I found I was polishing my glasses on Zack's bedspread. I stopped. 'We've got to do something.'

'I don't see what we can do about it,' said Zack. 'They're his kittens.'

'But——'

'Oh, push off, will you, Soppy, I've got to practise.'

I called him the rudest word I knew and slammed the door behind me. Why did I have to be cursed with an older brother?

Rug was in the kitchen, sitting on the worktop with one leg in the air as he washed his bottom. I picked him up and hugged him. He's sort of mottled brown and part Persian and has that very long hair that manages to be both rough and soft at the same time. If we forget to groom him he gets knots and has to have them cut out till he looks like a sheep that's missed being shorn and is losing its fleece in lumps.

9

'You'd look after them, wouldn't you?' I said to Rug. Rug purred. I suppose he's not the brightest of cats.

I was not doing my homework at the bottom of the garden when Mum arrived home. I had to revise for end-of-term exams, and I'd laid my notebooks out in matching patterns but I was finding it impossible to concentrate.

The garden is big—far too big, my parents said when we moved in, but they liked the house so bought it anyway. The garden is in two bits, divided by a hedge about a third of the way down. We (Mum, mostly) keep the bit of the garden near the house more or less tidy, but the bottom part is left to itself. It's my favourite place for when I'm feeling cross. There's a gap through the hedge that only I—and Rug—are small enough to get through without a struggle so usually I'm left in peace.

There's a weedy pond, with lilies, and frogs in season, and sometimes dragonflies. There's a bench, spattered with lichen and bird droppings, and behind it a wooden hut, its windows grey with spiders' webs. And almost smothering everything, like something out of 'Sleeping Beauty', is a tangle of honeysuckle and clematis and climbing roses.

I tried for the hundredth time to read about the Romans, but all I could think of was the kittens. I've always wanted a kitten to play with. All right, I know, I've been told often enough, a kitten soon grows into a cat, but it's an experience I've never had and just because an experience doesn't last long doesn't mean you shouldn't try it, does it? What about all the things grown-ups do that they think are so important? What about sex, for instance? Mum got a bit carried away, once she'd found the bottle to tell me about these things (as if I didn't already know) and said sex was a moment's pleasure and a lifetime of doing other people's washing.

I know there's Rug, but he's older than me, positively geriatric, and interested only in eating and sleeping. I've tried him with balls of wool and catnip mice and ping-pong balls. The only time he showed any interest was with a clockwork kangaroo that turned somersaults: he shot off behind the sofa and refused to come out.

So here I was, able to offer the kittens an ideal home where I would cater for their every whim, large garden offering amazing play potential, and I knew exactly what my parents would say. 'Who pays the mortgage?' they would demand. 'Who works to pay the bills?' And that would be the start of another lecture on why they say what goes round here and how I made quite enough mess already without getting more animals to add to it.

But more than anything else it was the thought of the kittens being drowned that I couldn't bear: being thrown into cold dark water, and sinking, and choking . . .

The first I knew that Mum was home was when the back door flew open. There was a shout of 'damned cat' and the door slammed shut again. I went through the hedge and found Rug sitting on the lawn, licking his tail with an injured expression.

11

Mum was wiping the worktop, which is white, except where a trail of pawprints led from the fridge to the windowsill. 'Bane of my life, this worktop,' she grumbled. 'Why couldn't it be mud-coloured?'

'At least you can see where he's been,' I said helpfully.

Mum snorted, threw potatoes into the sink and rummaged in the drawer.

'Mum . . . you know Tracy Wetherall?'

'Now where's the peeler gone? What about Tracy Wetherall?' Mum works as a receptionist at the Health Centre and knows almost everyone in the area.

'She's got these kittens . . .'

Mum, finally finding the peeler, started scraping. The first potato was rotten right through. 'Look at that!' She threw it in the bin and started peeling another.

'. . . and they're going to be drowned.'

'Not now, Sophie.' Mum had her eyes shut. 'Not now. I've had a long day and I'm tired and I can't be doing with Tracy Wetherall's kittens right now.'

I was going to argue but thought better of it and went back down the garden. Presently there was a shriek from the kitchen and a little later a smell of burning.

Eventually the microwave pinged and I was called in to tea. Dad was home, watching the television news and reading the evening paper at the same time.

It was spaghetti bolognese, one of those ready meals, and not quite enough to go round. I didn't ask after the potatoes. The television showed pictures of people in tears and Zack slurped his spaghetti and Mum told him to eat it properly and she and Dad told each other what rotten days they'd had at work.

As soon as Zack had finished he said, 'Can I get down?' and went upstairs. The din from his guitar mixed with the noise from the television.

As soon as Mum went out to the kitchen to make a cup of tea I grabbed the chance to get Dad on my side. 'It isn't right, is it, Dad,' I said, 'for people to drown kittens?'

'Drown kittens? Well, no, they shouldn't let their cats have kittens if they can't look after them. It's simple enough to get them neutered.'

'Yes, but *drown* them, if they've already got them?'

'No, of course not. There's more humane ways of putting them to sleep.'

'You mean killing them. It's not fair, is it, not giving them a chance?'

Mum came back carrying mugs of tea just as I felt I might be getting somewhere. 'She's on about some child at school whose cat's had kittens.'

'Five of them, and they're ever so sweet, and her dad's going to drown them because they cost too much to feed.'

'Well, they are expensive,' said Dad. 'And there's the vet's bills as well, and it's incredible how much they eat, I remember when Rug was a kitten——'

'Dad! They're going to be drowned tonight!'

'Well, I'm sorry, but there's nothing *we* can do about it. We can't interfere,' he said.

13

'We could at least have one, though, couldn't we? I mean, Rug can't last much longer and we need a cat to keep down the mice.'

'Really, Sophie, how can you be so heartless? Poor Rug, what a way to talk about him.'

That made me really cross. Calling *me* heartless when it was them who were condemning the kittens to a watery grave. I was starting to say how unfair they were when Dad said, 'Ssh, I want to listen to this,' and turned up the volume on the television. It was the local news, about some kids who'd gone on the rampage in the shopping precinct. Thousands of pounds of damage. 'It's those yobbos off the Hill again,' said Dad. 'It'll put insurance premiums up.' The Hill is this big problem estate. All the town's trouble-makers seem to live there. Dad's always warning us never to have anything to do with people from the Hill.

By the time the item was finished I'd thought of another line of attack. 'It would be good for Rug,' I said, 'to have a kitten for company. It'll give him an interest in life, keep him young.'

'Give it a rest,' said Mum. 'The answer's no. Anyway, we're going on holiday next month.'

'That's all right,' I said. 'I'll stay at home and look after the kitten. And Rug. It'll be much nicer for him than having Mrs Jones come in to feed him.'

'Of all the ungrateful—' Dad had gone all pink. 'When I think how hard I work so that I can take my family abroad every summer . . .'

He went on. And on. Anyone would think we

14

enjoyed going on holiday. Enjoyed getting sunburn and food poisoning and bitten crazy by mosquitoes and plagued by loud louts who always get the best places by the pool and then spending the rest of the year paying the Access bill.

'Come on, Sophie, your father's had a hard day and so have I, let's have a break now, can we?' Mum kicked her shoes off and leaned back in her chair.

From beneath the table came the sounds of Rug being sick. 'That bloody cat!' wailed Mum.

'I think it's time I did some revision,' I said.

CHAPTER TWO

I went outside and kicked the garden wall. I wasn't going to give up, and I had a nasty feeling I knew what I had to do next, only I wasn't sure I had the courage. Then I thought of the kittens all trusting, not knowing what was going to happen to them. I went down the road to Tracy's house, trying to think what on earth to say.

Tracy's parents were washing up. They seemed a bit surprised to see me and more surprised when I didn't want to go and join Tracy out in the back garden. At least the kittens were still there, in their tea-chest.

'Mr Wetherall,' I said, taking a deep breath, 'please don't drown the kittens.'

'Huh?'

'It's not fair. They ought to have a chance.'

'Well, needs must, you know. I can't afford to keep that lot.' Mr Wetherall peered suspiciously at a saucepan and gave it an extra scouring.

'No, but you mustn't kill them. I'm sure we could find homes for them.'

'No, we tried that with the last lot.'

'That's right,' said Mrs Wetherall, stacking plates in the cupboard. 'I was talking to your mum in the Health Centre today. Everyone as wants a cat round here has got one.'

16

'Then why do you let your cat have kittens?' I said. Really, people are so stupid.

'I don't hold with neutering,' said Mr Wetherall. 'It's not natural.'

'But *you* don't have babies all the time,' I said.

The Wetheralls stopped what they were doing. 'The cheek of it!' exclaimed Mr Wetherall and took a step towards me.

I didn't think it was going right. 'Excuse me,' I said, 'I have to be . . .' And I went.

Back in my bedroom I jumped on the pillow for a while and told myself I wasn't going to cry. Then I blew my nose and polished my glasses. It was going to be dark soon. Problems, problems.

When I can't sleep sometimes, well, if I'm honest, quite often really, if it seems really dark when I shut my eyes, I make up stories. Red hot needles under my fingernails wouldn't make me tell what they're about, but anyway I'm always very heroic and rescue someone. And now, first chance for a real rescue and all I wanted to do was hide under the bed. And if I did that how would I ever be able to face myself again? So . . .

First I rolled up some clothes and made a body shape under the bedclothes. Then I looked out of the window. I ought to climb down a rope made of sheets but I'd just made the bed look right and anyway it was a duvet. I decided to go out the front door.

I carried my shoes, but in any case my feet didn't

make a sound on the thick carpet, at least none louder than the gunshots from the lounge. 'We're coming out!' shouted the television, but the lounge door remained shut.

The first stars were coming out as I ran down the road towards Tracy's house.

At first I was frightened my parents would see me, call me back. Then as I turned the corner there were other things to be frightened of.

I might as well admit I've always been afraid of the dark. When I was a toddler my parents bought me a nightlight, a toadstool with gnomes, and turned the main light off.

It was awful. The gnomes crawled round the toadstool, whispering to each other and looking at me from the corners of their eyes. And beyond the little pool of light was a great sea of darkness where anything might lurk.

I had nightmares every night for weeks. At last my parents gave up trying to save on electricity and let me leave the main light on. That was all right, so long as I checked under the bed and in the wardrobe before I went to sleep.

Sometimes I used to hear my parents talking about it on the landing, after they'd tucked me up for the night. 'Perhaps it's because her eyesight's bad,' Mum said. 'Sometimes she sleeps with her glasses on.'

'She'll grow out of it,' said Dad.

But I didn't.

'I think it's an Ancestral Memory,' Zack said once.

He'd been reading some book. 'She thinks she's a caveman hiding from the dinosaurs.'

'Dinosaurs died out millions of years before man evolved.' Dad read books too.

But I knew better than any of them. If you can't see, then you don't know what might be there. I kept the light on, and carried on checking under my bed.

Now, as the darkness came crawling out of the gutters, the houses hid behind their curtains. Shadows oozed over trees and cars. Things lurked, waiting to pounce. Then I heard footsteps behind me, soft, shuffling footsteps. I ran.

I didn't stop till I reached Tracy's street. There was a man standing on the pavement, just standing there. A match flared as he lit a cigarette. I nearly bolted back home, till I thought of the kittens.

So I crossed the street, away from the man, quiet as I could and tiptoed along the side of the houses.

The alley was black as anything. I felt my way down it, my hand on the wall beside me. Something rustled.

By now I had my eyes shut so I couldn't see how dark it was. My heart was beating so loud that I couldn't hear anything else. I kept walking, feeling stones sharp through the soles of my shoes, my hand scraping along the wall.

The wall ended. I opened my eyes. I was standing on the track along the canal. The moon was reflected on the water. I looked around but couldn't see anyone. I walked along the track, the long grass slapping my ankles.

The obvious place to hide was the old lady's garden. The fence was no problem, with a gap wide enough to slip through. The thick bushes were more difficult. I scratched my skin, snagged my clothes, got all sticky with something cold and damp. In the end I thought I'd pushed my way far enough. I leaned against one of the few bushes that wasn't covered with thorns and got my breath back.

I could see quite well now in the moonlight. The canal looked quiet and innocent. Just by my nose, glistening among the leaves, tentacles twitching, was a snail. Now I looked there were dozens of them, all slipping along silently, and slugs oozing. Right in front of my eyes a spider twirled down from a twig and began to spin its web. I wouldn't have minded so much if only they had made some noise about it. Every bush seemed to writhe with silent munching and stalking and stickiness. I was waiting for something to fall down my neck.

Far off, a train hooted. A car started up and drove away.

I tried to forget the creepy-crawlies. There were other things to worry about. Worst possibility, I might be too late. The kittens might already be at the bottom of the canal. I looked at my watch but the moon had gone behind a cloud and I couldn't make out the time. It didn't seem that late, though. The houses on the far side of the canal still had lights on.

Then I thought, how was I going to get the kittens out of the canal? I'd seen a video about lifesaving at school; you weren't supposed to jump in to save people, you should pull them out from the bank. Anyway, I couldn't swim. But the banks were steep and I had nothing to pull the kittens out with.

A branch would help. I looked around for something suitable but it was all leaves and twigs. Then I saw a dead branch lying on the canal bank. Just the thing. I was about to go and check it out when I heard a door open.

Footsteps crunching on the garden path. The gate creaked. It was Mr Wetherall, carrying a cardboard box. He looked around, then crossed the bank. There was a splash. He turned and went back towards his house.

I fought my way out of the undergrowth, hardly noticing the brambles fighting back. Through the fence. I could see the box floating, tipping to one side. I grabbed at the dead branch. It wouldn't move, rooted or buried in the earth. I tugged at it, hard as I could, but it stayed stuck. At least it was something to hang on to. Clutching it, I slithered down the bank, leaned out over the water. My fingers just touched the box. Slowly it swirled, settling deeper in the water. I strained further, scrabbling frantically to pull it to the bank.

There was a sharp crack, a jerk, and I think the branch must have broken because then I found myself in the water.

There was water in my nose, my mouth, drumming in my ears. Suddenly I realized I was going to die. I couldn't believe it. It couldn't be happening. Then I saw moonlight again and felt air gasping into my lungs and my arms and legs were panicking away as if they didn't belong to me and flailing at the ooze that slipped away like feathers flying. I bumped into something and grabbed it. I'd like to say I knew it was the box and I heroically rescued it but at the time I didn't know what it was till somehow my foot caught against something firm and I slithered and slopped and, I'm not sure how, found myself spluttering on the bank. I spent a while just being sick. Then it dawned on me that what I was being sick on was the box with the kittens in.

Inside was a wet black mass, but bits of it were sneezing. I took the kittens out one at a time. They didn't look like kittens, their fur all plastered down. They coughed and sneezed and complained: or four of them did. The fifth didn't move. It was all limp and floppy in my hands. I wondered if I could possibly try mouth to mouth with something so small? In desperation I shook it. Suddenly its mouth opened and its body convulsed. It was sick, then sat up and tried to wash itself.

I realized one of the reasons I couldn't see a lot was that my glasses were all over weed. At least I hadn't lost them. Unravelling the weed I tried to think how best to get the kittens back. I didn't fancy putting them back in the box but there was nothing else to carry them in. Then I discovered one of the kittens was missing. I found it glaring suspiciously at a beetle, and put it in with the others.

But the box had had enough. As I started to lift it the bottom fell apart. I'd had enough too. I burst into tears. The kittens climbed out of the remains of the box.

After a while I stopped jumping up and down and collected the kittens together again. They wouldn't stay where they were put, kept wandering off to look at things. I stuck them inside my sweatshirt and went home with my chest seething.

I didn't have time on the way back to be scared of the dark. My teeth were chattering, my feet were squelching and the five sodden kittens in my sweatshirt were scratching me to pieces. I wrapped my arms round my waist, afraid of a kitten slipping out and me not noticing. Then I slopped on down the road.

When I got home I realized I'd come out without a key. The back door was usually kept bolted in the evenings, since neighbours had been burgled while they were watching television. I kept my fingers crossed and crept down the side passage.

There was a light on in the kitchen and water gurgling into the drain. Pressed up against the wall I could hear movements inside, footsteps and the chink of china. The clunk of the biscuit tin. Chocolate digestive, I remembered. Suddenly I was starving. The kittens wriggled.

At last the light went out. I counted to eighty-seven, until I couldn't wait any longer, then tried the door. It wasn't locked. I whisked inside, through the kitchen, then stopped. The lounge door was opening.

Rug came out into the hall and sniffed.

I shot past him, up the stairs and into my room. I emptied the kittens out of my sweatshirt on to my bed and pulled off my wet clothes. They were all stuck to me: it was like peeling an orange. I climbed into my dressing-gown and felt a bit better.

The kittens looked awful, all in a soggy heap. I went to fetch a towel, but the bathroom was occupied. There were sounds of splashing and a gust of some manly fragrance. Zack must be in the bath. I got a clean towel out of the airing cupboard on the landing, the biggest I could find, and promised myself a bath later. I smelt rather strongly of canal.

I thought it was ungrateful of the kittens to struggle as I tried to dry them. One of them bit me and another disappeared under the wardrobe.

Zack was still in the bathroom. I decided that as soon as my parents were asleep I'd take the kittens down to the garden shed. They'd be safe there. While I was waiting I thought I might as well get warm in bed, though I'd have to be careful not to fall asleep.

I checked under the bed as usual—no monsters, only cats—and burrowed in under the duvet. Something came to sit on my head.

CHAPTER THREE

I was woken by something trying to climb into my ear. I jerked up, dislodging a shower of kittens. They looked at me reproachfully, pink mouths opening in protest. One or two, by concentrating, managed to squeak.

They were hungry, obviously. Being half drowned had given them an appetite.

It was still dark, just after three by my clock. I went to listen at the door. The kittens clustered around my feet. It was all quiet. Gently I opened the door and slipped out.

The kittens slipped out with me.

They didn't run off, just sniffed around the landing. I kept picking them up and putting them back inside my room. But it was as if they were on elastic, every time I put them in they bounced back out again.

After some minutes of scoop, toss, boing, squeak I got fed up and as I caught each kitten I parked it on top of the dressing-table. It was a long jump from there.

I'd managed to get four of them teetering on the edge of the dressing-table when I heard my parents' light click on. I closed my door fast and stood against it. There was still a kitten on the landing. I kept my eyes shut and prayed.

I heard my father's footsteps, then the bathroom door, then splashing. Where *was* the kitten?

The loo flushed. Footsteps again. My parents' door closed.

I waited a moment, then peered out. Four kittens, having parachuted down from the dressing-table, peered out with me. There was no sign of kitten number five.

This was all getting a bit much. It was the middle of the night and I wanted sleep. I looked round my room for a suitable cage.

There was a large cardboard box full of toys I'd grown out of. I took all the toys out, one by one at first, so as not to make a noise, then got bored and tipped the whole lot out—Lego bricks, broken cars, bits of doll, and jigsaw pieces. There was also my favourite hair scrunchie which I hadn't seen for ages.

I'd put three kittens in and had caught the fourth when they figured out how to climb up the side of the box and all swarmed out again.

By this time I was beginning to wish I'd left them to drown.

Then I had an idea. The bottom drawer of my dressing-table was deep and the inside surface was plastic. They wouldn't be able to climb out of that. I tipped the clothes out and shovelled in the kittens. That'd fix them.

Then I went to look for kitten number five.

All the doors upstairs were closed. So were the doors downstairs. My parents had a thing about fire. The kitten was not in the hall, not on the stairs, not on the landing. Not in the bathroom.

The only place it could be was in my parents' bedroom.

I listened at their door. Not a sound. Then, a small scampering noise. A creak and rustle as someone turned over in bed. A half-sigh, half-yawn. Then silence again. Then, softly, thump.

Very, very slowly I turned the handle. Very, very slowly I pushed the door ajar. I dropped onto hands and knees and peered in. I could just make out the kitten sitting on the bottom of the bed, washing.

I could creep in very quietly and hope the kitten didn't move before I got there. I could make a grab for it. I could go away and forget it and pretend it was nothing to do with me.

Then I had this brilliant idea. I amaze myself sometimes. I took the belt off my dressing-gown and, holding one end, flipped the other towards the bed. The kitten watched as I pulled the belt slowly back. Then, as I flipped it in again the kitten leapt from the bed. It crouched, hindquarters waggling.

A third flip, and the kitten charged. I hauled the belt in with the kitten attached, grabbed it firmly by the scruff, pulled my parents' door closed and ran back into my own room.

I looked longingly at my bed but the drawer kept squeaking and I didn't think it was going to stop. I plodded downstairs to the kitchen.

Rug prrped politely from on top of the boiler, turned

over and went back to sleep. I opened a can, emptied it into Rug's bowl, and crept back upstairs.

Liberated from the drawer, the kittens plunged at the food, standing in the dish and on each other and slurping the food up like vacuum cleaners.

I looked out into the garden. The moon had vanished and there were things tapping in the wind. My toes curled at the thought of taking the kittens down to the shed in the dark. Well, I didn't have a torch. I thought I'd take them in the morning, early. Before Mum and Dad woke up.

'Sophie! Come on, get up, it's a quarter to eight.'

I opened my eyes. There was a kitten looking at me from the chair and three in a row on the windowsill. The room stank: I had forgotten to provide a litter tray. I leapt out of bed and was ambushed by the fifth kitten springing out on to my toes. I pulled on my school clothes fast as I could and ran downstairs. 'Hello,' said Dad. 'Bye.' He went.

'Hurry up, Sophie, you'll be late for school,' said Mum.

Zack started to sniff. 'There's a funny smell in here,' he said.

'Has that cat——' Mum looked round suspiciously. Rug, washing on the sideboard, looked up with an injured expression.

'No, not that sort of smell,' said Zack. 'Fishy, more.'

'Nonsense,' said Mum; but she was sniffing.

'It's Zack's hair gel,' I said.

28

'More like your feet,' said Zack. 'At least I wash.'

'You mean you're always hogging the bathroom so no one else gets a chance.'

'Don't start that now,' said Mum. 'What's that noise?' A rumbling had broken out overhead. It sounded as if the kittens were wearing Doc Martens.

I was trying desperately to think of some suggestion when a car started up outside. By the time it had moved off the kittens were quiet. 'I can't hear anything,' I said.

Mum shook her head. 'I give up. Has anyone seen the cat's bowl? I can't find it anywhere.'

'He's eaten it, I expect,' said Zack.

'Very funny,' said Mum. 'Come on, Zack, you'll miss your bus. Bye, Sophie, don't be late.' The door slammed behind them and the car started up in the drive. Zack's school is the other side of town and Mum gives him a lift half way. I have to walk.

Silence. I sagged with relief.

First I phoned the school, using my gruffest voice. 'Mrs Marriott here. I'm taking Sophie to the dentist. She'll be in a little later.'

Then I opened a can of cat food. Rug approved: he always appreciates a second breakfast. I gave him some in a saucer, then emptied the rest on to a dinner plate and carried it upstairs.

As I went upstairs my bedroom started to howl, like a very small wolf. When I pushed open the door a sort of black tornado hurtled out at waist height and landed around my feet. I put the plate down before they ate me alive.

While they were eating I tried to clean the carpet. I wasn't very successful, the smell just seemed to get stronger: cat pee, disinfectant, and canal. I opened all the windows and hoped the pong would go in time.

The kittens settled down to wash. It was the first time I'd been able to look at them closely, and I started to pick out some distinguishing features. One had two white socks, and another a small white bib. A third, as I saw when it rolled over, had a white spot on its belly. The other two were all black and however much I tried I couldn't tell the difference.

It was about time they had names. I felt they should form a set, but couldn't think of any sets of five. Three, yes, or four, but not five. Then I found I was humming the song Zack was always playing: 'Parsley, sage, rosemary, and thyme'. White-socks could be Parsley, white-bib Sage, spot-on-belly Thyme; while the two I couldn't tell apart could be Rose and Mary and it wouldn't matter too much if I got them muddled up.

I sat and watched them play for a while, then remembered I was supposed to be at school. I used the drawer to carry them down to the shed, made them a bed out of a cardboard box and a sweater I didn't like very much and filled a seed pan with earth for them to use as a litter tray. When I shut the door on them they were sniffing around their new home and Parsley was trying to climb the spade.

Carrying the empty drawer back to my room I caught sight of the clock: quarter to ten. I shut the door on the mess, grabbed my bag and went off at a run.

By the time I got to school it was past ten o'clock and there was a police car in the yard.

I slid into my place as quietly as I could. The lesson was geography, with Mrs Steele explaining rainfall; but although people were quiet—they wouldn't be anything else in Mrs Steele's lessons—I could feel there was something going on.

'What's happened?' I whispered to Laura. 'Why the police car?'

Laura looked sideways at me, all shiny with pleasure at being able to tell someone who didn't know. 'Tra—' she said and stopped dead as Mrs Steele turned from the board.

I thought I'd explode with frustration. Tra what? Tracy? What about Tracy? Accidentally-on-purpose I dropped my pen, bent to pick it up and while I was down there peered towards the back of the classroom, at Tracy's desk. It was empty.

I felt a nudge at my ankle. Laura started to write something. By leaning back in my desk I could just read it. 'Tracy Wether—'

'Laura, perhaps you would explain to the class what is meant by the phrase *rain shadow*?'

I was really worried now. It couldn't surely have anything to do with the kittens, could it?

Finally, in the rustling as photocopies were handed round, Laura managed to get it out: 'Tracy Wetherall's been kidnapped!'

It was so unexpected that I hardly knew how to react at first. Things like that didn't really happen, they

31

belonged to television dramas, with suitcases of money and car chases and gunshots and a handsome hero rescuing the beautiful heroine, still immaculately made up despite having been locked in a dungeon for three days. I tried to see Tracy as the heroine but it wouldn't work. Adventures aren't real.

I had almost convinced myself that Laura had made it all up when an altogether nastier idea came trickling into the back of my mind. Like twisting the focus on a camera so that a different image grows sharp. Snatches on the news: real policemen making statements to the press, real parents making appeals, a photograph of a smiling child, the newsreader's sombre voice. Things you were warned about but didn't really understand: never take sweets from strangers, don't go into the woods, never accept a lift from someone you don't know. The underneath of life, as if the world was thin as eggshells and if you put a foot wrong you'd fall through to where there were things worse than the creatures of monster movies, worse than creeping ghosts or fungus that turned bodies to gloop. Things without shape or voice or reason: darkness, waiting.

I felt sick. I picked up a pencil and began to draw kittens all down the margin of my exercise book.

And then, lunchtime, there was Tracy swaggering down the corridor. She was immediately surrounded by her mates, all wanting to know why she wasn't chained up somewhere while her captor issued ransom demands.

'What are you doing here? You're supposed to have been abducted.'

'You're supposed to be chained up with rats and thumbscrews and—'

'It's all a con. She made it all up.'

'I did not,' said Tracy indignantly. 'I escaped. I was very brave, the police sergeant said so.'

'Go on—'

'What happened?'

'Well . . .' Tracy lowered her voice so only those closest could hear. That didn't include me.

I went to the library. I'd been going there anyway, to get a book about looking after kittens.

I found one and sat down to read it, but it was hard to concentrate. Had the kidnapper leapt out from hiding? Or followed Tracy, slowly getting closer and closer? Or had he just looked like an ordinary passer-by until he grabbed her?

I took a deep breath and went back to my book. It was full of photos of cute kittens sitting in baskets or hanging by one paw from a ladder, but when I'd looked at the pictures I started to read. The text was all about tapeworms and roundworms and fleas and earmites and dreadful diseases with long names and you must wash your hands after touching a cat lest you catch ringworm or toxoplasmosis and you must never, never let them sleep on your bed.

I closed the book. The cover showed a family of kittens, wide-eyed and fluffy, and I tried not to think about things burrowing in their fur or wallowing in their guts.

I decided to read the book later. It was time for lunch—though I wasn't sure I felt like food.

CHAPTER FOUR

At the end of the afternoon there were more cars than usual outside the school gates—so many, in fact, that the whole road snarled up and a traffic warden appeared to add to the chaos. Word must have got about, and worried parents were arriving in droves to collect their children.

My parents weren't among them—well, they couldn't be, really, they'd be at work. I was surprised, though, hurrying home to see the kittens, to find Tracy walking along the road in front. I broke into a run to catch her up, and Tracy spun round, looking alarmed, then stopped when she saw who it was.

'Where's your police escort?' I asked. I was dying to ask her what had happened, but of course I couldn't.

'Ha ha.' Tracy kicked a can along for a while, then trod on it and booted the remains into the gutter. 'Dad said he'd come but I wasn't going to hang around.'

'Aren't you scared?'

''Course not.' Tracy sounded definite enough but I wasn't really convinced. 'Wish I'd never said anything,' Tracy went on. 'Next thing, Dad'll be saying I can't go out on my own. I don't want to be stuck at home all the time.'

'Mm,' I said, not wanting to stop the flow.

'Just along here it was. By the bridge. This car stopped and the passenger door opened and this guy leaned over and asked me the way to the post office. He made out he couldn't hear me and he kept getting right and left muddled and I was leaning in the car door explaining all over again and suddenly he grabbed me and tried to pull me in.'

That gave me shivers down the spine. 'What happened?' I asked, when I'd finished gasping.

Tracy shrugged. 'I hit him,' she said casually. 'He was wearing glasses and I hit him on the nose. He let go and I ran off. I wouldn't have said anything only I ran straight into Mrs Steele and she told me off for rushing around. Then they called the police and my mum and dad and I had to make a statement, give a description and all that.'

I heard a car slowing down behind us and jumped. 'It's all right,' said Tracy, grinning. 'That's not him. It was a white car, Sierra or something like that.'

We got to the corner where to go straight home I turned left and Tracy right. I thought I ought to offer to walk Tracy's way, because Tracy must really be frightened even if she said she wasn't. But then I'd have further to walk, on my own, and I was scared too, and anyway I wanted to get back to the kittens.

While I was thinking about it a white car stopped beside us and the passenger door swung open.

'Hi, Dad,' said Tracy, getting into the car.

Mr Wetherall leaned over and recognized me. 'Oh, it's you,' he said. He didn't sound that pleased to see me. 'Hop in, I'll give you a lift home.'

'Sophie lives in Westbury Avenue,' said Tracy, doing up her seat belt.

Mr Wetherall grunted, pulling out into the traffic. 'You should have waited,' he said. 'I told you I'd come.'

'I told you I didn't want a fuss.'

'I don't care what you want. While that man's around you're not going out on your own.'

Actually he didn't say 'man', he used a word I hadn't heard before, even from Zack in a bad mood. I sat on the edge of the back seat wishing I'd walked home on my own. Tracy and her father carried on arguing.

'What number?' asked Mr Wetherall as we turned into Westbury Avenue.

'Ten,' I said.

'I'll pick you up in the morning,' said Mr Wetherall as we stopped outside the gate.

'No, really—'

'It's no trouble. We'll be passing.'

Life's peculiar sometimes, isn't it? I smiled sweetly at the man who had tried to murder the kittens and thanked him for the lift and went off to see how they were.

They were hungry. In fact, they were starving. As I went up to the shed they were howling and when I opened the door they erupted round my feet in a seething indignant mass.

Thank goodness I was first home. It took a while to sort the kittens out—get them all back in the shed, feed them, clean up the mess, fill their tray with new earth. Eventually they had eaten and washed. I sat down in a reasonably clean corner of the shed and they all came and sat on me. Favourite position was on top of my chest, just under my chin, and they wriggled and jostled and overbalanced, all trying to wedge themselves in. They all purred impossibly loud and they were soft and warm and full of spikes. My bottom was going numb from sitting on the wooden floor, my neck stiff from being twisted away from the edge of a shelf and someone's claws were sticking into my shoulder. But I wouldn't have moved for anything. All those round black pupils in baby-blue eyes gazed at me unblinking and I had fur up my nose and felt like God.

Till I heard Mum's voice calling, 'Sophie! Sophie, are you home?' Obviously I was, I'd left my school bag in the hall and the kitchen door open, but I couldn't risk Mum coming to look. I tried to unwind the kittens, who didn't want to move either. I disentangled some and put them down but as I was dislodging the others the first ones climbed back on. I might have been there for ever, but Parsley discovered a leaf and they all went to watch as it attacked him.

'Sophie! Where are you?'

I opened the door of the shed and right outside was Rug. His eyes were hard points, his tail jerked convulsively, his lips curled over a growl. The kittens, with pleased expressions, trotted up to say hello. Spitting like a young volcano Rug spun round and ran, lily pads bobbing in the waves as he flew over the pond.

'Sophie!'

I shoved the kittens back into the shed and followed Rug through the hedge.

'*There* you are,' said Mum. 'Whatever's the matter with Rug?' Tail like a brush, he was agitatedly washing, still growling.

'Perhaps he's seen a ghost,' I said. 'They do say cats are sensitive to psychic phenomena. Did you want me?'

'Oh . . . no. Just wanted to know where you were. Put the kettle on, will you? Do you want a cup of tea? Or there's some hot chocolate and I bought some doughnuts so long as you don't let them spoil your dinner. I'll just . . .' And she wandered off upstairs.

Strange, I thought. She's not usually so solicitous.

But it only lasted till she opened my bedroom door.

'Sophie!!!'

I put the bag of doughnuts down and went to my room. Mum was standing there, furious. 'Look! Look at this . . . mess!'

The bottom drawer of the chest was lying on the floor surrounded by a pile of sweaters. Covering most of the rest of the carpet were the things that had been in the cardboard box, which lay there broken from when I must have tripped over it. My duvet cover, usually cream with pale pink roses, had gone a curious shade of mud, while in a heap by the door festered the clothes in which I had fallen into the canal. The smell still hadn't gone.

'Sorry, Mum.' I edged in front of the dressing table, over which led a trail of small paw prints outlined in some nameless muck. 'I'll clear it all up. Now.'

Mum breathed and seethed for a moment, then marched out, slamming the door. I set to tidying. I didn't think I'd be getting a doughnut.

When the usual smell of burning announced that tea might be nearly ready I went downstairs to earn back some credits by laying the table. Dad was in the lounge, reading the evening paper as usual while the television talked to itself in the corner. Except that the paper wasn't rustling as usual: he had folded it into a square and was actually reading it.

Tea was bangers and mash surrounded by gravy thick enough to eat with a knife and fork. Mum had tried to liven it up by pushing the more burnt ends of the sausages into the mound of potato so that they stuck out. 'Like maggots from a skull,' said Zack.

Conversation dried up after the weather forecast, when the local news came on. The first item was about a factory closing down; but then, suddenly, there was a reporter standing outside my school. The camera moved off him and started to show pictures of the roads along which I walked home, then switched to a bald man in a suit captioned Detective Inspector Something. He agreed this morning's incident could have been much more serious and urged parents to be vigilant.

When the piece ended Dad pressed the remote and silence fell.

Till Zack said, 'What a wally. Fancy trying to kidnap Tracy Wetherall.'

'You don't even know her,' I said. I was furious with Zack for making out it wasn't important.

'I do too. Her brother's in my class. She tried to chat me up once. I told her where to get off, silly cat.'

'Zack!' said Dad.

'Well she is too,' muttered Zack.

'Wasn't it Tracy had the kittens?' asked Mum by way of diversion.

'How appropriate,' murmured Zack. 'What did I say?'

'Her dad brought me home,' I said. My turn to change the subject. 'He said they'd give me a lift tomorrow.'

'That's nice of him,' said Mum, looking surprised. 'I was trying to think how I could take you to school, but we're short-staffed at the moment, with Glenda being on holiday, and someone has to open up . . .'

'That's all right then,' said Dad. 'You're not to go out on your own, mind, not till this maniac's caught. You got that?'

'Yes, Dad,' I said, wondering how I was going to get to the shop to buy some cat food. A lot of cat food, the amount they ate . . . It wasn't going to be long before someone noticed that Rug's tins were disappearing fast.

'Why don't we get a Rottweiler?' asked Zack. 'A really big vicious one? Sophie needs protection . . .'

'No,' said Dad.

'But, Dad, it'd be great . . .'

'No,' said Mum. 'I'm not having any more animals in this house. I have enough trouble with you lot.'

I went to do the washing up.

* * *

Later, in my room, I thought of doing my homework but picked up the book on the care of cats and kittens instead. I was flicking through the pages on pests and diseases when a flea landed on the book. I caught it between my fingertips and squashed it; but when I opened my fingers it jumped onto the bed and vanished. I crawled up and down the duvet looking for it. Then it (or another one) appeared on my leg. This time I squashed it between my fingernails. There was a small cracking noise and a blob of stuff like pus popped out. I wiped away the remains and went back to the book.

I read that a small kitten has a stomach the size of a walnut. It should have small, regular meals, five a day.

I panicked. I didn't see how I was going to manage that, except at weekends. They were at least two meals behind already. I ran downstairs and out into the garden.

I'd been reading about the importance of hygiene in raising kittens as well, so I washed their plate out in the pond before opening another tin. As usual, they fell on it and in five minutes had eaten themselves spherical.

I sat on the bench soaking up the evening sun. It was warm and quiet, the scent from the honeysuckle heavy and sleepy. The kittens didn't seem to want to run off: they sniffed around the shed and the pond, learning the area. They all tended to do the same things at the same time. When Parsley took exception to a twig, they all jumped. It was always Parsley who took the lead, and when for a while he dribbled a stone they all followed, chasing the tail of the kitten in front.

I'd been so busy kitten-watching I'd almost let it get dark around me. I caught two pairs of wrestling kittens and shut them in the shed, then looked around. One was missing: Parsley, of course.

I called (in a whisper), 'Puss puss puss.' No sign. I listened. After a while there was a rustle, off to the right, and a scuffle. I crawled under the bush. There was an agitated flapping and a crescendo of squawks as a blackbird erupted out of the undergrowth. Then silence.

Parsley must have gone further. I looked through the hole in the hedge, dreading seeing him trotting over the lawn in full view of the house. No sign. No sign of him in the neighbouring gardens either.

Then I thought of the pond. Surely not—I ran to it, stared in, holding my breath. There was no sodden black bundle floating on the surface . . . He wouldn't have *sunk*, would he?

I leaned back against the shed, trying to keep calm. 'Puss puss puss,' I called again.

Muffled squeaks responded politely from inside the shed.

I told them to shut up.

One squeak sounded louder than the rest. Then I realized it wasn't inside the shed, but on top of it. Looking up I saw Parsley grinning down at me.

I chucked him in with the rest of the litter and went back to the house, wondering how, short of levitation, the kitten could possibly have got on to the roof of the shed.

Reaching the kitchen door I found it was locked.

My first impulse was to bang on the door, rather loudly, until rescued. But Mum and Dad would want to know what I was doing outside and I couldn't think of any reasonable explanation for sitting in the garden while darkness fell. They would think I'd been out somewhere, defying the ban.

It would have to be Zack. I was bound to regret it: I'd be putting myself at his mercy and he would take full advantage of it. But I didn't have any choice.

His bedroom overlooks the garden. His window was open, and he was playing the guitar, practising chords. I picked up some small stones and threw them. It always looks easy when they do it on the television. My attempt was pathetic: the stones went nowhere near Zack's window, and one bounced back off the wall and hit me on the head. I tried again, several times, till eventually I got my eye in and some pebbles went in through the window. But the chords carried on.

I kept trying, but Zack just kept on playing. Pudding-head. I looked around for a more noticeable missile. I didn't dare try a bigger stone, it might break the window. There were some tomatoes leaning rather drunkenly in a gro-bag against the wall: they were just starting to ripen. Still, Mum wouldn't miss one or two. I aimed carefully.

The tomato flew in through the open window: I heard a plop as it landed. The guitar stopped, but Zack still didn't look out.

I picked another, aimed and hurled. This time the

tomato going in through the window met Zack, on the nose, as he leaned out.

'Ssh!' I hissed, putting my finger to my lips.

Zack looked as if he was about to say what he thought of people who went round throwing tomatoes through windows. Then he paused. 'What's it worth?' he asked.

'Let me in and I'll tell you,' I said.

'Tell me first.'

'Zack, *please!*'

He leaned more comfortably on the windowsill and looked down at me. I looked back up at him, trying to look pathetic while really wanting to throttle him. Abuse of power, it is. Just because he's bigger than me. For a while we just stood there looking at each other till finally Zack relented.

'All right,' he said, as he opened the kitchen door, 'What's the big secret?'

I locked the door on the dark and filled the kettle. Zack stood there all supercilious and smug, smirking down at me and I was thinking, it's not fair, I can never be as old as him. I had been going to let him into the secret. Really I had. Only there had been too many times when I'd told him things, and then he'd gone and told Mum and Dad though he'd promised he wouldn't.

There was after all a left-over doughnut. I bit into it, the jam spurting down my chin. 'Shan't tell you,' I said.

'You little toad! You promised!'

'So?'

'I'll tell Mum you were out in the dark.'

'Prove it,' I said. 'She'd never believe you.'

'You little——' Zack dived at me and I dodged past and ran upstairs, crashing into my room and slamming the door. I stood against it, holding it shut while Zack beat on the outside, yelling and shoving.

'What on earth's going on? Zack, stop that noise, for goodness' sake!' Mum sounded really ferocious.

'Sophie Marriott, you're a waste of space!' Zack howled outside, then slammed off into his own room.

I slumped on the bed, and a flea jumped onto my knee.

CHAPTER FIVE

Next morning Zack wasn't talking to me. I could feel
him watching me closely, though, looking for a clue to
what I'd been doing outside in the dark. But I had set
my alarm clock for six o'clock and fed the kittens while
everyone else was still asleep. I ate my cereal nice and
slowly and was ready for school, teeth brushed, even
hair combed, when Mr Wetherall's car hooted outside.

'Bye, Mum,' I said, smiling sweetly.

Zack ground his teeth.

The feeling of triumph soon wore off, though. I sat in
the back of Mr Wetherall's car listening to him and
Tracy sniping at each other and wished I didn't have to
be there, that the day was already over, and that I had
never heard of kittens.

For a start I was feeling really tired. I seemed to have
spent the whole night being driven mad by creepy
tickling sensations and sudden nips when the fleas, since
cat was unavailable, decided human would have to do.
Then I was worried the kittens would have to wait too
long for their next meal: there was no way I could get
home at lunchtime, and after school Zack would be
watching, wanting to catch me. The kittens might die
of starvation. Or start eating each other. And anyway I

had almost run out of cat food, or rather Rug had, and I couldn't think how I was going to get more, since I wasn't allowed out on my own. Perhaps I should have told Zack, got him on my side, only I wasn't sure I could trust him. One thing I was sure of, though: he wouldn't be on my side now.

And then, to cap it all, it was Friday and straight after break was P.E.

'Now mind you wait for me after school,' said Mr Wetherall when we arrived.

'Lot of fuss about nothing,' grumbled Tracy, getting out and slamming the door.

'Thank you very much,' I said, shutting my door so carefully that it didn't catch right and I had to shut it again.

The lesson before break was maths, which I'm really rather good at, though I've learned to keep quiet about it. It's bad enough having to wear glasses without being seen as a swot as well.

Mr Rogers was in a bad mood and gave us a lecture about being such a dumb lot. I wasn't listening and when Mr Rogers suddenly asked me a question made the mistake of giving the right answer.

'Well, I'm glad *somebody* has a grain of intelligence,' said Mr Rogers.

I wish teachers had a grain of intelligence. What a thing to say.

After break I retreated to my usual dark corner of the

cloakroom and set out my P.E. kit so that I could scramble into it with maximum speed and minimum exposure. I don't like my body. I don't like seeing it myself and I hate other people looking at it. Not like some—Rebecca, for instance, who undresses in the middle of the aisle and keeps her clothes off till everyone has had a good look.

I wasn't fast enough. 'Hey, look at all those scratches,' shrieked Rebecca. 'What's she been doing?'

'Been down in the woods,' said someone.

'With a boy!'

'Shame on her!'

Everyone was laughing. Rebecca, wearing nothing but knickers, was poking at me. I yanked down my blouse and felt for my glasses. They had gone. Someone had taken them from the bench and hidden them. I'm really short-sighted; if I haven't got my glasses I can't find them.

They all laughed some more and were still laughing when they ran out to the field.

It took ages blundering round the cloakroom to find my glasses. So that when in the end I caught up with the others I was shouted at for being late and made to run three times round the field and then I was screamed at for not running fast enough and screamed at some more for stopping to get my breath back and when I finally joined in the rounders I was all over the place and a ball hit me on the chin and I was run out and howled at for letting the team down.

* * *

Lunchtime people were still busy talking about The Kidnap. The girls, anyway. The boys played football same as always. The first years kept gathering around the gates and screaming every time a white car approached. I noticed Tracy was sitting by herself not talking, which isn't like her. I sat and watched ants walk round and round the rim of a plantpot, while the boys ran round after their ball and the girls ran round after their pretended frights and Tracy just sat and stared.

Then in the first lesson after lunch, quite suddenly, Tracy burst into tears. Mrs Steele went out with her and came back on her own talking of delayed shock. I thought, I bet she's going home. Lucky thing.

But about twenty minutes later I was sent for.

'Couldn't go without you, could we?' said Mr Wetherall. 'I said I'd look after you, didn't I?'

Tracy had stopped crying but was still silent. 'No need to go straight home, is there?' said Mr Wetherall. 'Tell you what, I've got to go to Tesco's, we'll go into the café there and I'll buy you a cream bun.'

I couldn't believe my luck. I could stock up on cat food and I'd even get a lift home with it. Then I realized I didn't have any money with me.

We went straight into the café when we got to the supermarket. Mr Wetherall prowled along the cake counter like a hungry lion. 'I think I'll have a cream meringue,' he said. 'What about you, Trace?'

Tracy didn't reply.

'Sophie, what would you like? It's all right, it's on me.'

The reason I was hesitating, though, was because I thought it was against my principles to take cakes from a kitten-murderer.

'Go on, have a Danish pastry,' he said. 'Apple or apricot or sultana?'

I couldn't make up my mind.

'Let's have them all,' said Mr Wetherall. 'Hey, look, rum babas. I used to eat them all the time. You ever had a rum baba, Trace?'

He heaped the tray with cakes, overflowing on to a second tray and the drinks on a third.

We unloaded the trays on to a corner table and suddenly Tracy started to giggle. We had so many plates we couldn't get them all on the table.

'Wade in,' said Mr Wetherall grandly, sitting down with a Bakewell tart perched on his knee. 'I bags the meringue.' It exploded in his face and a crumb lodged in his eyebrow.

Stuff principles, I thought, and stuffed myself with cake. It's not that often I get the chance.

'What do you call a cross between a sheep and a kangaroo?' asked Mr Wetherall.

'I don't know, what do you call a cross between a sheep and a kangaroo?' said Tracy, humouring him.

'A woolly jumper!'

You wonder where grown-ups get these jokes, don't you?

Still, you have to be polite. 'Do you know what a cauliflower is?' I asked.

'Go on,' said Mr Wetherall.

'It's a cabbage with a college education.' Well, *I* like that one.

Tracy burped, though that might have been the Coke. 'Thanks, Dad,' she said.

Mr Wetherall smiled at her, patted her hand, then cried, 'Eat up! Come on, you haven't finished.'

'I couldn't eat another thing,' said Tracy.

'Me neither,' I said.

'All right, I'll ask for a doggy bag.'

'We haven't got a dog,' objected Tracy.

'Henry likes cake.'

'Who's Henry?' I asked.

'Our cat.'

I said, 'Surely your cat's a female?'

'The man we got her from was having us on,' said Mr Wetherall. 'He swore blind it was a tom, then a few weeks later she had kittens. By that time we'd got used to him . . . *her* being Henry.'

'Henrietta,' mumbled Tracy thickly, patting her stomach.

It was very confusing: how could Tracy's father be kind and buy cakes and drown kittens?

We collected a trolley and went into the supermarket. 'Anything you want to get, Sophie?' asked Mr Wetherall.

I wasn't sure what to say. In the end I said, 'Yes, but I haven't got any money with me.'

'Oh, that's all right, I'll lend you some till you get home.'

I heaped up a basket with Whiskas. My parents

taught me never to borrow, but they *were* Mr Wetherall's kittens after all . . .

When we got home Mr Wetherall got out to open the boot and searched through the carrier bags looking for my cans. Mum's car was in the drive.

'I'll just get the money,' I said, trying to take my shopping from him.

'No, I'll carry it, it's heavy.'

I ran to the house with Mr Wetherall following behind. I used my key, hoping Mum wouldn't hear.

'There you are, Sophie.' Mum was in the hall. 'It's very kind of you to give her a lift, Mr Wetherall.'

He was standing there holding the bag of Whiskas, exchanging polite remarks. I rushed upstairs to fetch my money. When I came down again they were still talking. I hovered there wondering how on earth I was going to exchange the money for the bag without Mum noticing. 'Was that the phone?' I said.

'I don't think so,' said Mum, and carried on with the conversation.

'Is that something burning?' I said.

'Oh damn, the onions.' Mum disappeared. I handed over the money, Mr Wetherall put the bag down. Mum came back and after a few last pleasantries Mr Wetherall finally left.

'Oh,' said Mum, closing the door and catching sight of the bag. 'He's left his shopping. Catch him, Sophie.'

I opened the front door and waved goodbye to the car till it drove off. Then I closed the door and said, 'Too late.'

Mum looked in the bag. Twelve cans of Whiskas looked back at her. 'How odd. Why did he bring that in? I'd better ring later to tell him it's here.'

'I'll do it,' I said. 'Is Zack back?'

'No, did you want him? He's got cricket practice. Oh, my God, those *onions*.'

Five minutes later I had changed out of my school clothes and was walking casually down the garden with the Whiskas concealed amongst my homework.

The shed was howling like several banshees and when I opened the door I was engulfed in black fur. Kittens clinging to various parts of me, I picked my way into the shed, which stank. It was wonderful, if overwhelming, to be so much appreciated.

It was only after I had cleaned up and after the kittens had eaten and washed and were starting to play that I noticed they were being watched: Rug was by the gap in the hedge, tail twitching, poised between flight and advance. The kittens took no notice of him. Eventually Rug settled down, paws tucked under. He stared unblinking, until two of the kittens rolled too close and suddenly he was gone.

Tea was late—'What with Mr Wetherall coming and everything,' said Mum, putting the plates on the table—and the local news was starting as we sat down.

There'd been more trouble in town, a gang fight outside a night club. Someone had had a knife. Two people had been taken to hospital and several arrested.

One of the people arrested came from the Hill. 'I knew it,' said Dad. 'Bunch of savages they are up there.'

'Disgusting,' agreed Mum. 'Streets aren't safe for decent folk.'

'Savages,' said Dad again. 'You make sure you don't go out on your own, Sophie.'

'Who'd want her?' said Zack.

I glared at him. He should have shrivelled to a crisp.

'Do you know, Mum, I think her squint's getting worse,' said Zack.

'What, dear?' asked Mum, without taking her eyes from the television.

I tried to kick Zack under the table, but missed.

'Behave yourself, Sophie,' said Dad.

Zack squinted horribly at me.

I imagined chopping him to pieces and feeding him to his own piranha fish. The image had a soothing effect. I asked Mum if I could vacuum my room after tea.

The vacuum cleaner was new, with all sorts of attachments cunningly concealed. I used them all, cleaning in every crevice with special reference to the bed. I could almost see the turbo boost devouring the fleas. Unfortunately it also devoured a ballpoint pen. The machine rattled for a few seconds and then, the case of the pen digested, spewed up the inside, like an owl regurgitating the bones of a vole.

It was dark by the time I finished. I drew the curtains, looking down the garden, patches of black chequered by windowlight. Somewhere beyond the hedge the kittens would be curled in a purring heap. The next day was Saturday: if I could only keep out of Zack's way I'd be able to spend more time with them.

I coiled up the flex of the vacuum cleaner, trying not to think of the fleas curled up in the fluff inside.

CHAPTER SIX

It was the best sort of Saturday morning. The sun was shining and Zack was out. I'd given the kittens an early breakfast and was dawdling over my own. I poured myself too many Rice Krispies and when I added milk they rose and settled all round the rim of the bowl. When I put my spoon in several dropped off onto the tablecloth.

It reminded me of that arcade game that has a whole fortune in coins perched on the edge of winning and when you roll another coin down the chute a scoop pushes them forward and if you've rolled just right your coin pushes off hundreds and you're rich. I added one Rice Krispie to the bowl and dipped the spoon in and out. Two Krispies fell off the edge. I went on adding them one at a time, dipping the spoon in and out . . .

'Sophie! What on earth do you think you're doing?' Mum was looking cross, holding a duster.

I started eating.

'I've got enough to do today without you adding to it.' Mum hates housework. She plugged in the vacuum cleaner and Rug asked to go out.

'Have you seen my hammer?' said Dad, coming in carrying a jar of nails.

'You're not going to mend the fence, are you?' asked Mum. She'd been asking him to do it for months.

''Course I am. If I can find the hammer. I've hunted high and low.'

'Cupboard under the stairs?'

'Not there.'

'Must be in the shed, then.'

I choked over my Krispies. 'I'll get it for you,' I said.

'No, you won't. You poured all that cereal, you just eat it.' Mum switched on the vacuum cleaner.

Dad opened the back door and Rug shot out. I shovelled the Krispies down as fast as I could as Dad went down the garden. He stopped to poke at a bush.

Maybe he'd get sidetracked. He usually did. I couldn't believe it. Why should he choose today of all days to mend the fence? He walked on, pushed his way through the hedge. I had to close my eyes.

Mum switched off the cleaner. Suddenly everything went quiet. I heard the shed door open. There was a shriek of pure terror. Then a shout. *'Sophie!'*

There was no escape. Mum was standing there with a saucepan in one hand and a tea towel in the other saying, 'What have you done *now?'*

Very reluctantly I went down the garden with Mum following.

Dad was by the shed, not so much holding the kittens as wearing them. They must have been feeling lonely and were pleased to have a visitor. There were two on his shoulders, two clinging to his arms, while the fifth was slowly climbing up his trouser-leg.

When he saw me Dad said, 'And how do you explain this?' He sounded really cross, despite having a kitten nibbling his ear.

I was still trying to think of something to say when behind me I heard Mum giggle. It was too much. I giggled as well.

'It's no laughing matter,' said Dad.

'Certainly not,' said Mum, relieving Dad of the kitten which had climbed on to his head. 'I suppose these are Tracy Wetherall's.'

I nodded.

'Then you can just take them straight back,' said Dad.

'No,' I said. 'No, I can't.'

'You'll do what your father tells you,' said Mum.

'No, no, you don't understand——'

'I understand you've gone behind our backs——'

'I couldn't help it. I had to save them.'

'No, really, Sophie, they're not our problem. You just take them back to Mr and Mrs Wetherall and apologize——'

'But I can't! Mr Wetherall tried to drown them! He threw them in the canal!'

'If he threw them in the canal how did they get here?'

'I went in and got them out.'

'You *what*?'

'It was Wednesday night,' I said. I couldn't think of any way out except a full confession. 'I waited at the bottom of their garden and then when it got dark Tracy's dad came and threw them in the canal in a box and I tried to pull it out but I fell in and I had to swim but I got the box out and they were all wet and nearly drowned and I couldn't let him do that, could I?'

Nobody said anything for a while. I almost began to feel a bit hopeful.

'We can't keep them,' said Mum. 'I have to admit they're very sweet but we can't keep them.'

'No way,' said Dad, untying his shoelace for Parsley to play with. 'No way.'

'We'll take them to the Cats' Home,' said Mum, as Rose (or Mary) licked her neck and purred. 'Now.'

Sitting in the back of the car clutching Rug's basket full of squeaking kittens I didn't know whether to feel most angry or sad or worried or relieved. Sad at having to part with the kittens, or angry that what I felt and what I knew was right was ignored, or relieved because they were an awful lot to cope with and I wasn't honestly sure if I would have been able to keep it up. Worried at what would become of the kittens: what was this Cats' Home anyway and could they be trusted to look after the kittens properly? I didn't really believe anyone else could care for them as much as I did.

I started to feel sad again but was interrupted by Parsley who had been probing a weak strand in the basket and now managed to get his head out.

I tried to push it back in but it seemed to be stuck. I made the hole a little larger and disentangled Parsley but as soon as I had stuffed him back into the basket there was someone else's black paw sticking out of another hole and when I had dealt with that Parsley was poking out again. I was still trying to put bits of kitten back into the rapidly disintegrating basket when we arrived at the Cats' Home.

It was a single-storey building that would have looked better with a coat of paint. From it came a chorus of miaows. I hugged the basket to my chest. I was not impressed.

We rang the bell, then, as no one answered, went in. The walls were covered with pictures of cats. A room on the left was marked Private: the miaowing came from there. On the right was a door labelled Office. Mum knocked and opened the door, but didn't go in: there didn't seem to be room to get in.

The office was the size of a middling sort of cupboard. It was piled high with crates of cat food and sacks of litter, amongst which was a desk, behind which was an intimidating glare. Peering round Mum, I managed to work out that the glare belonged to an elderly woman with very short grey hair. 'No room,' she barked.

'Miaowoww,' agreed the invisible cats.

The kittens squeaked.

'They're not ours,' said Mum. 'My daughter rescued them.'

The woman was working through a card index on the desk. 'Where from?' she asked, taking a red asterisk from a box and sticking it on a card.

'From the canal. Someone tried to drown them.'

The woman eyed the asterisk closely. Evidently it

showed signs of leaping from the card: she slammed her fist down on it. The cans bounced.

'There's still no room,' she said.

Miaowow*ow*,' said the cats.

'But——' said Mum.

'Look,' said the woman. She pointed to a chalkboard divided into 48 numbered boxes. There was something written in every box: 3) Ad.m.ging. 10) F. tort. 9 mths. 17) F. tab. ad. + 3 K. (2 b/w m.* + 1 b.f.) 6 wks. It looked like algebra.

'All full,' said the woman. 'The asterisks are booked but I've got seventeen kittens and four adults waiting to come in. I'll put you on the waiting list if you like.'

'How long would it be?' asked Dad, trying to assert himself round the doorpost.

The woman sniffed. 'Two weeks maybe. Depends how fast these are homed. What have you got anyway?'

She took the basket from me and took out a kitten: Sage, who had been known to nip. Sage didn't dare. The woman held him up and inspected both ends. 'He's too young to home,' she said. 'Eight weeks they need to be. I doubt he's six yet.' She tickled Sage behind the ear and he licked her hand. She put him back with the others. 'Bring them back in a fortnight,' she said, slapping bits of sticky tape over the damaged bits of basket.

'While we're here,' said Mum, 'can we have a look round? Our cat came from here. He's fifteen now. You're Mrs Ferris, aren't you? I've been trying to remember your name.'

'Can't remember yours,' said Mrs Ferris. 'Would probably remember the cat.' She ushered us in through the door marked Private.

The miaows got louder. I was overwhelmed: deafened, stifled by the smell, stared at by hundreds of yellow eyes. The walls were lined with cages, and in every cage was at least one cat. In several there were sets of kittens with their mothers, climbing the mesh and begging to be stroked.

'Don't touch,' said Mrs Ferris. 'Spreads diseases.'

I stuffed my hands in my pockets to keep them under control and worked my way along the rows of cages. The kittens were all cute. The adult cats varied from the elegant—even snooty—to the battleworn to the downright peculiar. But they all managed to make it perfectly clear that they would rather be elsewhere.

All except 3) Ad. m. ging. Mrs Ferris opened his cage door and he climbed out into her arms: carefully, as he had only three legs and one eye. He nestled into her iron bosom and purred loudly. 'He's my baby, aren't you,' said Mrs Ferris fondly. 'Ginger was a stray,' she explained, 'knocked down by a car. No one would take him so he stays here.' Ginger rubbed his cheek against hers and smiled.

By the time we got back in the car we were all feeling slightly stunned. 'Can't think how she copes with working there,' said Dad, riffling through the glove compartment for some toffees and passing them round. 'No wonder she's loopy.'

'Can we keep them?' I asked through a mouthful of toffee. 'Till they come here?'

Mum and Dad looked at each other. Dad turned and looked at me. 'I suppose,' he said, 'we'll have to.'

On the way home we stopped at the chemist's on the High Street. Mum made jolly conversation with the traffic warden who appeared out of nowhere and started to tell us off and stayed to coo at the kittens till Dad came out of the chemist's carrying a very large cardboard box labelled Disposable Nappies (Size 3).

'The kittens will be out of the way in here,' he said, putting the box in the boot.

I didn't say anything. I thought they'd find out soon enough.

Zack was livid. Partly because he'd missed it all: he'd returned from a music lesson to find that he'd forgotten his key and everyone was out and he had to wait an hour and a half till we got back, then to discover that I had been found out and that there were kittens and he was the last to know.

'Huh,' he snorted, and went off to his room to express his feelings playing his guitar especially loudly and especially badly.

The kittens had spent a tiring morning and after a brief exploration of the box, a small snack, and a queue to use the litter tray they wriggled themselves into a heap, closed their eyes, and went to sleep.

Mum started on some serious housework from which Dad escaped by going into the garden where he sat on the bench in the sunshine and thought about mending the fence. I was made to help Mum. I pleaded homework but was overruled. 'Have you forgotten grandfather is coming tomorrow?' said Mum.

'Oh, *no,*' I said. I had managed to forget. Grandfather (he insists we call him that) is just about my least favourite person. Apart from Zack, of course. Grandma walked out on him twenty years ago and ever since he's been concentrating on proving he can manage quite well without her, thank you. He keeps his flat as clean and tidy as an operating theatre and expects us to do the same. Of course, we don't. Mum wears herself to a frazzle trying to please him, and she never does—except that I suspect that what really pleases him most is being able to find fault with us.

I had to feel sorry for Mum so I only grumbled a bit as I picked up a duster. 'Can't Zack help?' I asked. It was worth a try.

'He's got to practise,' said Mum, starting to clean the windows.

Upstairs the guitar shrieked.

I was just beginning to feel I was making progress when the kittens woke up.

I kept putting them back in their box, but I couldn't watch them all the time.

There was a scream from the kitchen when Mum found a kitten buried in the pile of washing she was about to put in the machine. 'I thought that shirt was alive!' she said, putting Thyme back in the box. Fortunately she didn't stop to count the kittens, so she didn't notice Parsley on top of the curtain rail. She went back into the kitchen.

I climbed on the table and unhooked Parsley very carefully—the curtains are velvet. By the time I had climbed down again the others were all out. I put them back into the box and gave them a duster to play with. Then I went to the loo.

They were all out again when I came back downstairs. Sage had turned on the radio by sitting on the button. Rose, Mary, and Thyme were having a tug o' war with the duster. Parsley had disappeared.

I decided I might as well let them potter. I carried on dusting.

Rose and Mary included the telephone in their wrestling match and succeeded in dialling out. 'Sorry,' said a bright female voice from the phone. 'The number you have dialled has not been recognized.' Rose (or Mary) peered anxiously into the receiver until Mary (or Rose) jumped on her, and Thyme jumped on both of them. 'Sorry,' said the phone. 'The number you have dialled—' I put the receiver back and removed Sage from under the tablecloth. There was another scream from the kitchen, where Mum had found Parsley in the tumble drier.

Tea was late again. We'd missed the news and the television was showing a game programme with people in multi-coloured leotards thumping their chests like gorillas and swinging on rings like overweight orang-utans. Zack thought it was great; Dad liked it when someone fell off; Mum ignored it, and kept getting up to run her finger along the tops of picture frames or to peer behind chairs.

'Give it a rest,' said Dad. 'The house is clean, your father can't expect more than that.'

'Oh yes, he can,' said Mum, breathing on a photograph and polishing it with her sleeve. 'You know what he's like.'

Dad cheered as a muscle-bound youth with a spray-on smirk was knocked from his perch by a shrewd thump in the guts from his opponent, and cheered some more as the opponent overbalanced and fell flat on his face.

'We'll have to do something about the kittens,' said Mum. 'They won't stay in the box.'

Dad looked round the room. There were no kittens to be seen, only a gentle purring from the box. 'They're all right,' he said.

'Only for the moment,' said Mum. 'They were all over the place this afternoon. They'll have to go back in the shed.'

'Better not. Go on, hit him—no, harder! That's it . . . No, I had a look, it's full of tools and chemicals and that, I'd have to clear it all out to make it safe.'

'What sort of chemicals?'

'Oh . . . weedkillers, fungicide, that sort of thing.'

'When did you last kill a weed? That stuff must be years old, you should get rid of it.'

'Easier said than done. It's got to be disposed of properly, you know, you can't just pour stuff like that down the drain.'

'Well, I still think the kittens would be better in the shed. At least for tomorrow.'

'Why don't we put them in the kitchen?' I said.

'Goodness, no. Father would have a fit.'

'I'll have them in my bedroom then,' I said. I think that was brave, considering the fleas.

'No, I'm not having animals upstairs.'

'They'll have to stay where they are then,' said Dad. 'Wake up, you daft haddock . . . Aaaah!'

The last contender did a bellyflop into the safety net.

After tea Zack invented a fishing-for-kittens game, dangling a cord into the box and hauling it up when he had a bite. Sometimes he got two or three at a time. I tied a piece of string to an empty cotton reel. Dad produced a large paper bag, which the kittens dived into, on to, and through. Rug sat on the sideboard and watched. Mum twitched.

About nine o'clock Dad had a call from a colleague at work. We all had to keep quiet and turn the volume on the television down, while he talked about output and targets and productivity and noted salient points. I noticed Thyme picking his way along the back of the sofa. He was watching Dad's pen, waving in the air.

Dad was concentrating so hard on his conversation that he didn't notice Thyme arrive in his lap: at least, not until the kitten took the pen in his mouth and went off with it.

Various other kittens joined in, dribbling the pen across the floor. I found another one and gave it to Dad.

Rug progressed from sitting on the sideboard to sitting under the table. Once or twice, as the kittens sprinted past, he almost joined in.

Quite suddenly the kittens were tired, so tired that wherever they were, in mid-game, they stopped and went to sleep.

Mum and Dad fell asleep too, so I didn't get ordered upstairs when the horror movie started. Zack sat with his eyes glued to the screen. I stroked Parsley on my lap and kept dozing off till I was woken up by the noisy bits with bullets and bombs and people's insides being splatted up the walls.

Till Mum woke in mid-murder and sent me to bed.

I left Parsley curled up on a cushion and went upstairs. Lying in bed I could still hear the television screaming.

CHAPTER SEVEN

I was right in the middle of this dream where I was running away from a man with a gun and every time I turned a corner there was a white car waiting to grab me when I heard Mum telling me to get up. I looked at the clock. 'It's only half past seven,' I said.

'Grandfather will be here at eleven,' said Mum, 'and I need you to help.'

The kittens had discovered the kitchen roll. I had to crawl round the carpet picking up shreds of tissue. I didn't even get any breakfast.

From the kitchen came the sounds of Mum going crazy over the cooking.

The telephone rang and Dad answered it. 'Oh, really? . . . Sorry to hear that . . . No, of course . . . Yes, we are . . . Of course, love to see you . . .'

Mum was hovering at the kitchen door, spatula in hand. 'Who was that?'

'My mother. They're going to see Aunty Ethel in hospital this afternoon. They say she's not getting any better. They're going to pop in on their way home, just for a cup of tea, they said not to do anything special.'

'Oh no, George, they can't. You know they don't get on with father.'

'Your father doesn't get on with anyone. They're my parents, I can't tell them not to come.'

Mum was about to argue but screamed instead. 'Sophie!' My fault again. Parsley was swinging from the curtain. I retrieved him and Mum went back to having hysterics in the kitchen.

I went back to picking up bits of tissue. Dad sidled towards the front door.

'They're not open yet,' snapped Mum, bobbing out of the kitchen. Sometimes I think she has ESP.

'I was just going to get a paper.'

'By way of the Rose and Crown, you mean. Sophie will get the paper. Here's some money, Sophie, run along now and can you get some carrots while you're there, I forgot to get any and father does like his carrots.'

'We said she wasn't to go out on her own,' said Dad.

'Oh . . . oh, all right, you go then, but for heaven's sake be quick!'

Mum started taping newspaper over the top of the kitten box.

'They won't be able to breathe,' I said.

'There's holes in the sides.' Mum went on taping.

The holes were slits for carrying the box. A black paw poked out of one, then vanished.

At eleven o'clock the doorbell rang.

Mum screamed. 'Oh no, there he is and me in my apron and your father not back. I knew I shouldn't have let him go . . . ' Still wailing she vanished upstairs. I supposed I'd better let grandfather in.

71

I could see him through the reeded glass in the front door, looking about ten feet tall. I adjusted my smile and opened the door.

'Ah, Sophia.' I hate being called Sophia. He stepped in and stopped to wipe his feet. He was wearing a dark suit with a white carnation in the buttonhole and carrying a Harrods bag. He always has a Harrods bag to carry his apron and slippers.

Mum rushed downstairs, tripping on the bottom step and almost falling.

'Take your time, my dear,' said grandfather. 'You almost knocked me over. Coffee in here, is it?' He walked into the lounge and settled himself in the best armchair, which happened to be the one next to the kitten box. I followed him in just in time to see a black paw emerge through the hole in the side. It couldn't reach.

'How are you getting on at school, Sophia?' he asked, unlacing his shoes and exchanging them for a pair of sheepskin slippers from the carrier bag.

I didn't have to answer because just then Mum came in carrying a tray. 'Here we are, father,' she said brightly. 'Coffee, your favourite brand, and almond macaroons, just as you like them. I made them this morning.'

'How kind. You'll forgive me if I move the chair a little? The sun is rather strong . . .'

I watched riveted as grandfather moved his chair back out of the offending sunshine and closer to the kittens. 'Macaroons, you say . . .' He took one and laid it on his plate, and the plate on the coffee table which by now was right next to the kitten box. 'You're looking a little worn, if you don't mind my saying so. A woman should look after herself, especially when she gets to your age, Jane.' He sipped his coffee and set it down next to the plate, his fingers reaching for the macaroon which wasn't there. I could have told him where it had gone, but didn't. 'Dear me, I was sure I—thank you, my dear . . .' Grandfather took another macaroon from the plate and bit into it. 'Mmm. Are you sure the almonds were quite fresh, Jane? It doesn't do to skimp on the ingredients . . .'

He put the half-eaten macaroon down on the plate while he drank his coffee. The paw appeared once more. The biscuit somersaulted from the plate and vanished.

This time I didn't offer another. I just enjoyed seeing grandfather look confused.

Resolutely he rose above it. 'And where is George this morning?'

'He's had to go and see someone about the car,' said Mum. Fibber. 'He's having trouble with it.'

'Indeed? I always feel one shouldn't have a car if one doesn't know how to maintain it. And Richard? Where is he?'

'Oh . . . Zack's revising. He has a maths exam tomorrow.'

'Then I suppose he must be excused. Still, I always think it's a pity to leave revision to the last moment, don't you? If things are done at their proper time there's no need for all this rushing to catch up.'

'More coffee, father?' Mum sounded as if she had her teeth clenched.

'No, thank you. You know I only ever have one cup. An excess of caffeine is detrimental to one's health.'

While Mum was trying to think of something to say there was a scuffling noise. Grandfather turned and looked at the box. Silence.

'And how is your hip?' Mum asked.

Grandfather cheered up, and launched into a tale of agony bravely borne, of hospital visits, incompetent physiotherapists, ignorant doctors, inefficient clerks, inane consultants. 'And what,' he said, reaching the climax of his story, 'what do you think I said to that?'

There was a sound of tearing paper and a small black head appeared. 'Mew,' said Parsley.

Fortunately grandfather was in a good mood. He put on his reading glasses, viewed the kitten and pronounced it rather sweet. He then took his apron from the Harrods carrier bag and escorted Mum to the kitchen, from where he could be heard continuing the saga of his hip in the intervals of telling her how to improve her cooking.

I was left with the kittens. I felt rather limp. Then I decided that anything was better than just sitting there, so I carried the box full of kittens down to my end of the garden and squeezed through the hedge. The kittens seemed pleased to have an outing and pottered around quietly. The sun was warm and smelt of green leaves.

I was drawing a map of Australia and marking in the cities and half thinking about going there on holiday when I realized something was going on. Nothing to do with the kittens, for once, they were just sitting looking interested. A movement in the bushes, a lot of insistent chirping. Then a loud buzzing and a blue tit landed on a twig just over my head, and carried on calling. Blue feathers, yellow feathers, one bright eye. Another buzz, an electric sort of sound, and another blue tit materialized, even closer. I could see where the feathers furled into each other. Both birds went on calling and suddenly there was another whirr in the bush. A young blue tit, obviously straight out of the nest, he hadn't combed his hair yet. He clung to the twig with one claw, looking ridiculous. One of the parents gave him a caterpillar. He was still trying to swallow it when two more of the brood arrived, each with that electric whirr and much excited cheeping.

'Sophie,' Mum shouted. 'I need some help in the kitchen.'

By half past twelve things were getting desperate. Lunch was scheduled for exactly one o'clock— grandfather's digestion required regular meals. There was no sign of Zack, of Dad, or of the carrots.

I had laid the table—best linen, best china, everything matched. The kittens had helped, getting under the tablecloth as I spread it, sitting on mats and removing spoons.

At quarter to one Zack appeared, shook grandfather's hand politely and asked how was his hip. Grandfather told him. Mum was muttering to herself—something about killing him. I didn't like to ask who was to be murdered. I removed Parsley from the table again.

At ten to one Dad came in, bringing neither carrots nor Sunday papers, but smelling rather strongly of beer. Grandfather made some pointed remarks about drinking and driving. As Dad didn't know he was supposed to have been out in the car he got rather indignant. Mum rushed in and out of the kitchen, her face shiny with exhaustion and sweat. I took Sage off the table.

At five to one the doorbell rang.

It was Dad's parents. 'We were a bit early for the hospital,' they said, 'so we thought we'd pop in. Oh, I see grandfather's here.'

They greeted him with a certain lack of enthusiasm. They couldn't have been more different: where grandfather minced, they surged, and they insisted we call them Bill and Enid. I let them kiss me with a fairly good grace—at least they meant well. Zack, though, had obviously prepared for this: Enid closed her eyes to kiss him and opened them as she felt her lips planted on a rubber mask of Frankenstein's monster.

She thought this was a very good joke. 'He's a lad,' she said, wagging her finger at him. 'Oh, are you going to have lunch?' she went on as she caught sight of the table. 'Don't worry about us. We've got sandwiches.' She and Bill sat side by side on the sofa and unwrapped paper packages.

Mum opened and closed her mouth a few times, looking a bit like Zack's piranha fish. Then she went into the kitchen.

The rest of us sat down to table. Mum came in, carrying the roast.

Grandfather leant forward: there was a speck of dirt on the snowy tablecloth. As he raised his hand to brush it away it started to crawl; then jumped.

'A flea!' he shrieked, leaping up and knocking into Mum, who dropped the roast.

'Surely not,' I said.

From the cardboard box came a disgusting smell. I dreaded to think what the kittens had just done.

Grandfather walked out. Bill and Enid sidled out. Mum and Dad had a row.

I heard it all from the stairs. And I heard when Mum telephoned the Cats' Home.

'First thing in the morning . . .' she said.

I went on upstairs. Zack's door was half open. 'Can I come in?' I said.

'Looks as if you are in.' Zack was sitting at his desk reading.

'They're going. The kittens. First thing in the morning.'

'Where to?'

'The Cats' Home. Mum rang.'

Zack looked up from his book. 'Really, you are naïve, Soppy!'

'Don't call me that! What do you mean, naïve?'

'The Cats' Home is full, right?'

'Yes.'

'Cats in every cage? No room anywhere?'

I nodded, not sure what he was getting at.

'Well then, where are the kittens going?'

'But Mum rang . . .'

Zack leaned forward. 'Where do you think the Cats' Home gets the money to run?'

'I don't know . . . The government?'

''Course not. Don't be daft.' Zack lowered his voice. '*Medical research.*'

'What do you mean?'

'Laboratories need animals for their experiments,' Zack explained patiently. 'They inject the animals with awful diseases, then inject them with different medicines, and watch how long it takes them to die. The Cats' Home sells spare animals to laboratories, and that gives it the money to run. Simple.'

I couldn't believe him. Surely it couldn't be true. 'You mean the kittens are going to be experimented on?'

'You got it.' Zack went back to his book.

I felt as if I was drowning. The piranha fish shuffled their jaws. I had to run to the loo to be sick.

It didn't take me long to realize what I had to do. It took a lot longer, though, to convince myself I had the courage to do it.

PART TWO

CHAPTER EIGHT

By evening the kittens, chemicals or no chemicals, had been banished back to the garden shed. Dad had gone to the pub, Zack to a friend's house to revise, and Mum to bed with a headache. For a while I stared at the television without seeing it and ate biscuits: then I made up my mind. I didn't have any choice. I'd started rescuing the kittens and I had to carry on with it. Though I wished I'd never heard of them. Anyway I was never going to speak to my parents again. I'd never forgive them for agreeing to let that happen to the kittens.

It was all quite easy. I fetched Zack's rucksack from on top of his wardrobe and packed a sleeping-bag, some cheese sandwiches, cans of Whiskas, a plate, and a tin opener. Then I took Rug's travelling basket down the garden to collect the kittens.

Finally I was ready. The house was silent. There was only Rug to watch as, carrying rucksack and cat basket, I opened the front door and went out. It was just getting dark.

Too easy: I looked round, almost hoping to be called back. But no one appeared to scold, 'Where do you think you're going?' There was no one around at all.

Night was trickling into the gaps between the houses

and my head was full of monsters. Only the fact that I was rescuing the kittens from a fate worse than drowning prevented me from bolting back indoors.

I set off down the road. The rucksack was heavy and the cat basket awkward: it kept banging against my knees. I changed hands and the kittens complained.

At the end of the street I turned left, towards the park. Cars passed, catching me in their headlights. On the far side of the road was the Rose and Crown. Dad was in there. As I went past a door opened, but it was only a teenage couple, the girl's high heels clacking.

I kept to the shelter of the garden walls, but still felt exposed as each car swept by. Dazzled by the lights, I couldn't see the colours of the cars, see which were white, when I had to hide. I just had to keep walking, changing the basket from hand to hand as it got heavier.

Then I heard a car slowing down behind me. I panicked, shrinking into the shadow of a tree as the car drew to a halt a little way ahead.

The passenger door swung open.

A woman got out, called 'Goodnight' and crunched away up a garden path. The car drove off and I heard the click as a front door closed. I started breathing again.

I went on till a door opened on the other side of the road and a woman appeared, carrying something. By the gatepost the woman stooped and shook something out on to the ground. Then she turned and went back into the house. The door closed, but in the room beside it a curtain twitched, leaving a chink of light.

I couldn't think what she was doing. I stood watching

from the shadow of a tree, waiting to see what happened.

The kittens sensed something first. They all peered up the road. Trotting into the glow of a street lamp came a peculiar-looking creature with long legs, a thick tail and a hump back. As it stopped by the gatepost the hump turned into a cub, jumping down. The fox nosed the ground and there were slurping sounds. Two more cubs appeared and joined in.

Along the wall came a cat, black and white, presumably, as I could only see bits of it, the rest was invisible. It jumped off the wall and moved in by the foxes, head down. The eating noises continued.

There was a squeaking as two of the cubs squabbled. A moth fluttered around the light.

Behind me I heard something snort. It sounded as if it wasn't sniffing, but blowing through its nose, really loudly. I was expecting something huge to come out of the dark, but it was just a hedgehog. It trundled closer, almost walking over my foot as it passed, then crossed the road, its legs much longer than I would have expected. I could hear its claws pattering on the pavement. It joined the other animals, legs folding away as it started to feed.

The light from the window disappeared as the curtain closed. I waited for a while, then realized the animals had gone, melted back into the darkness. I was beginning to feel like a creature of the night myself. The darkness was something to hide in. The trouble was the other creatures hiding there, creatures with fangs. Or weapons.

The way to the park seemed much further than it did in the daylight. I turned into a road where the lamp-posts were further apart and the spaces between them ink-black. No cars went by; there were just their humped shapes lurking by the kerb. I tried closing my eyes, so I couldn't see how dark it was, then nearly screamed as a hedge leapt out at me.

Then I heard footsteps behind, following me, quick hard taps and a rapid ticking. I ducked down behind a car as on the opposite pavement a man walked into a patch of lamplight, a spaniel at his side. The dog stopped, turned its head towards me, sniffing. I could feel it gobbling my scent. Then the man tugged the lead and their footsteps clicked away into the night.

At the top of the road were the park gates, padlocked. There was a notice giving the times of opening and saying that a bell would be rung half an hour before sunset. I went on past the gates to where two railings had been bent aside. There was just room to push the basket through. I took off the rucksack, squeezed through the gap, then turned to pull the backpack after. As I straightened up a bush seemed to explode.

It took me a while to realize it was only a pigeon. It had scared me half to death. I picked my way out of the flower-bed and paused to get my bearings.

The sky was clear and the moon was up, almost full, floating among swathes of stars. Zack would have been able to tell me the constellations. I could see the park laid out around, lawns sweeping up to the left, down to the right. At the bottom of the hill was the lake, dark with lilies, and at the far side the Grecian temple.

I turned towards the temple, but kept to the edge of the park, following the line of trees. On the moonlit lawn I would have felt as exposed as a fly on a dartboard.

As I got near the lake something splashed. The lilies rocked, the water flickered from black to silver to black. There were waves of some flowery scent.

I stopped outside the temple. Suddenly it occurred to me it might be a trap rather than a refuge. I had been thinking I could hide there, but now I just stood, staring into the shadows, thinking someone—something— might have thought of it first, might be crouched invisible, waiting. I listened, but I could only hear my own heart beating, blood rushing past my ears, my breath juddering in and out. Somewhere far off an owl hooted. I crept forward, trying to ignore the cold fingers running down my spine.

There was no one there. I was almost sure there was no one there.

In the temple was a stone bench. The ground underneath it was sandy and dry to the touch. I spread the sleeping-bag out and crawled into it. Propped up on one elbow, I opened the basket and the kittens, grumbling, jumped out. They sniffed around, pattering in and out of the darkness, bristling, whiskers on edge. But they didn't go far, and soon settled down in the sleeping-bag, wedging themselves in underneath my chin. There was an agitated tone to their purring. 'Don't you worry,' I whispered to them. 'Don't you worry about a thing.' I repeated it like a mantra, as if by reassuring the kittens I could reassure myself. But all the time I was saying 'Don't you worry' there was this big block of terror sitting at the back of my throat.

I knew I shouldn't have done this and I had no idea where to run to or how to save the kittens or myself. I was sure I'd be dead by morning, swallowed up by the night full of noises: scrabbling, sniffing, invisible things hunting. My breathing seemed terribly loud and I huddled over the kittens trying to quieten their purring. My heart seemed to be racing and then I couldn't feel it at all. I thought I was already dead. I was vaguely aware of a rough tongue licking my neck. I clutched the soft fur and murmured 'Don't you worry' till I felt myself falling into the dark.

CHAPTER NINE

I woke feeling ridiculous. It was light and I was still alive and I'd been silly to get into such a state.

Till I looked towards the doorway and saw the monster standing there.

It was an enormous black dog, shaggy, with the muzzle of a wolf. Head down, it sniffed. Yellow eyes gleamed as it padded towards me. Its jaws were parted, teeth shining, as the huge head thrust into the sleeping-bag.

Then a kitten crouched by my face spat horribly and swiped the dog's nose. The dog jumped back, looking shocked, and a whistle sounded and someone called. In a flurry and a leap the dog was gone.

I wriggled out of the sleeping-bag, showering kittens everywhere, and went to the doorway. The big black dog—which looked smaller now I was no longer lying underneath it—was lolloping after a man in a donkey jacket. Birds poked around in the grass, a squirrel scratched, and the sun shone. Life seemed brighter, though I still had no idea what to do.

The kittens pointed out that they were still waiting for breakfast, so I opened the rucksack.

Looking for the tin opener I discovered why the rucksack had felt so heavy: in one of the pouches were a hand-held computer game and Zack's Walkman. Amazingly, both had batteries that worked.

While the kittens munched, I listened to the radio, ate a cheese sandwich, and tried the computer game. The object of the game seemed to be to fly a spaceship through meteor clouds and hostile attacks, but I couldn't work out how to zap the aliens and kept being exterminated. In the end I threw the game back in the rucksack.

The Walkman pip-pip-pipped and started on the eight o'clock news. It was all bad: people being killed from fighting and earthquakes and accidents. Though the announcer tried to make it sound harmless and jolly, and rounded it off with a jingle.

None of it seemed real. The early morning sunshine was sharp on the grass, birds twittered, flowers bloomed. Kittens around my feet hoovered up the crumbs from the cheese sandwich.

The man in the donkey jacket must have opened the gates. The park was filling up with dogs, towing their walkers on leads, or trotting free to sniff and challenge and chase and run away. I thought it was time I moved, before any other dogs investigated the Grecian temple.

I discovered the kittens had been whiling away the time by chewing through the straps of their basket and there was now no way of doing it up. I was really cross, till I thought that the kittens would be better off in the rucksack. The basket was very conspicuous. If they were in the rucksack, so long as they kept quiet, nobody would notice them.

I stuffed the sleeping-bag into the carrier I'd used to wrap the sandwiches, packed everything else into the side-pockets of the rucksack, rounded up the kittens and set off. I sang along to the Walkman when I passed someone so as to hide the faint mewing from the rucksack.

I still didn't know where to go. It seemed, though, a good idea to go somewhere. The park was too close to home. As I went out of the gates I saw a bus and ran to catch it.

The bus was crowded and I had to squeeze in next to a fat woman with a shopping trolley. With the sleeping-bag on my lap and the rucksack on top of that I could hardly move. The woman avoided my eye and looked cross, as if I was taking up too much room. Very pointedly she moved up about half an inch and stared out of the window.

Then the kittens started complaining again. Scrabble, scrabble, squeak, squeak. I could feel the woman peering suspiciously out of the corner of her eye. I draped myself over the rucksack and jerked along to the music on the Walkman. The woman sniffed and went back to staring at the street.

Then what I'd been dreading happened. The most awful smell came out of the rucksack. The woman turned and glared at me. It was too much. I got up and went to stand by the door. Behind me I heard her say, 'Shouldn't be allowed,' and someone else said, 'Disgusting,' and, 'Why isn't she in school?' I got off at the next stop.

I didn't know where I was. There were no shops, only houses and trees chopped off at the top like fists. I went down an alley-way where there was no one about and got the kittens out of the rucksack. Luckily I'd lined it with the newspaper from the basket. Three of the kittens had managed to sit in the mess and I used all the tissues I had cleaning them up. Then I looked for a bin to get rid of the newspaper but there wasn't one, so feeling very guilty I stuffed it behind a wall and fled before anyone complained.

After a while I came to some shops. On the corner was a vet's surgery. I went in.

The waiting-room was full of people and dogs and cat baskets, but there was no one at the counter marked Reception. I sat down between a Dalmatian and a poodle and put the rucksack between my feet. The dogs sniffed at it, one on each side.

I had been thinking I could persuade the vet to take the kittens, but there was a notice-board on the wall covered with postcards all appealing for good homes for kittens, all claiming to be fluffy and adorable. Fat chance the vet will take this lot off my hands, I thought. Then I had another thought. I feel really ashamed of this, but I was getting desperate. I could just go and leave them, like people dump babies sometimes.

I was half-way to the exit when a voice said, 'Excuse me, is that your rucksack?' I turned to see a woman pointing. I stood there clutching the sleeping-bag and saying, 'I was just going to get some fresh air,' and feeling myself go hot because she obviously didn't believe me.

Just then the phone rang and the receptionist came out of a side door. She talked to me at the same time as the person on the other end of the telephone, which was a bit confusing, but she did agree to put up a notice about the kittens. 'I can't promise, mind,' she said. 'Bring him in between nine and ten tomorrow—There's always more kittens than there are homes—Don't give him anything to eat after eight o'clock tonight—I should ring the other vets if I were you—No, you should be able to pick him up about four—Here, I'll give you the phone numbers . . .'

I hadn't really meant to abandon the kittens, I told myself as I went down the road. Not *really*.

I was in the sort of rotten mood that needs a chocolate bar to put it right, so I went into a shop. One side was stacked with sweets, newspapers, and videos dripping blood and screams, while the shelves on the other side were full of poppadams and mango chutney. The window was covered with cards with things for sale.

I bought some chocolate and asked how much it was to advertise in the window. '20p a week,' said the woman behind the counter.

It seemed a bargain. 'I've got to find homes for some kittens,' I said. 'You wouldn't like one, would you? They're very pretty.'

She smiled, but shook her head. 'My son is allergic. Would you like some paper to write your advertisement?' She found me a card, and lent me a green felt-tip pen, and watched as I wrote 'Five adorable fluffy kittens, black, six weeks old, need good homes,' and added the first vet's phone number. I gave her 20p, saying, 'One week will be enough.' It had to be.

I sat on a wall and ate the chocolate and felt a bit better. The rucksack had gone quiet. When I looked the kittens were all curled up together sleeping. Hoping they'd stay that way I looked for a telephone.

The other vets agreed to advertise the kittens, so that was all right.

I had been half hoping that someone else would want to use the phone, because I knew I ought to ring home and I didn't want to. Nobody did, so I looked in my purse hoping I'd have run out of change, but I hadn't.

I watched a fly cleaning its legs on the glass while I rehearsed what to say, then called my number.

After two rings the answerphone cut in. I couldn't believe it. They should have been waiting by the phone desperate for it to ring. They weren't. They'd just gone to work as usual. They didn't care.

I was so angry I slammed my fist against the glass and squashed the fly. The mess stuck to my hand and I had to scrape it off, feeling even worse because I'd killed it and yelling 'Beast!' not knowing who at.

Things are a bit blurred then, till I found I was banging into people and realized I was at the bus station and saw, of all people, Mrs Steele. Panicking, I jumped onto the nearest bus, which had its engine running.

The driver asked where to, and I said all the way, not knowing where, and he charged me almost all the money I had left.

As I sat down the bus started off. I saw the woman who I had taken for Mrs Steele and of course it wasn't. She'd be in school now. So I'd panicked for nothing. Still, I didn't care anyway.

The bus drove on for what seemed like hours. I couldn't work out where it was going but thought it didn't make any difference.

Then the bus began to go even more slowly, grinding along in low gear as it struggled uphill. There were no trees along the streets now, just tatty houses, all the same.

The kittens started to squeak and scrabble around in the rucksack. Luckily there was no one sitting near enough to take any notice, and soon after the bus lurched to a halt and the driver switched the engine off.

I waited for everyone else to get off first. What with one thing and another it had only just occurred to me where I might be.

Stepping off the bus I looked round. There was a row of small shops and on the far side of the road a low grey building with several windows boarded up and graffiti everywhere and orange letters spelling out 'The Hill Community Centre'.

The other passengers had disappeared. Parked nearby was an old Cortina, one corner propped up on a pile of bricks. I remembered Dad saying, 'Barbarians they are up there. Barbarians.' There was hardly anyone about, though, except an Alsatian dog nosing through the gutter.

If I'd had the money I'd have got back on the bus, but

my purse was practically empty. I was desperate for a drink, though, and I had enough for a can. The kittens were making a terrible racket, so I propped the rucksack up in the shop doorway and kept looking round while I was waiting to pay to make sure no one stole it. What I didn't bargain for was the Alsatian.

It was hidden by a pile of crates till I opened the door and there it was pawing at the rucksack.

I expect it was the stupidest thing I could have done, but I did it without thinking. I grabbed the rucksack, and the dog came with it. No warning, just a blur and then its teeth locked into the sleeping-bag and I was jolted backwards and fell against the shop window. I must have been screaming, and a man appeared and hit the dog with a bottle and it let go and ran off.

'Effing dogs,' he said, and then to me, 'You all right?' though he didn't seem very interested and went off saying to a woman with a baby, 'Effing dogs. Shouldn't be allowed.'

As it happened, I was all right. No blood, I mean, though I couldn't stop shaking and there was a big rip in the sleeping-bag and I was desperate for a loo.

There'd be one in the Community Centre. I hesitated, but not for long, because I didn't really have a choice. Feeling as if I was approaching Enemy HQ, I crossed the road.

I met no one, though, and ran down the corridor and found the Ladies, which wasn't very clean but was still a relief.

Sitting on the loo I looked to see if the kittens were

all right. They were determined to get out and scratched my hand when I tried to stop them. I did the rucksack up again and sucked the blood from my fingers. Ungrateful little whatsits.

As I was about to leave the cubicle I heard someone come in. Two women. One went into the cubicle next to mine while the other leant against the wall. I could see her feet under the door.

'Police were up my way again last night,' said the woman in the cubicle over the noise of clothes being pulled down.

'Regular event, innit?' said the other.

''Sright. Every night, near enough. I said to old Trev Jones, you know, lives round the back of me, comes for a good gawp every night, I said I'd sell him a season ticket.'

The woman outside lit a cigarette. 'So what was it this time?'

'Oh, it was those kids again. Wayne Watkins, and that boy from the offy, and him they call Flash Harry and a whole bunch more, they got this beat-up old blue van, drove it to the top of Britten Hill, God knows how they got it there, puffing and banging it was. Anyway they get it to the top, turn it round and give it a good shove. Went down the hill like a ruddy rocket, you never see anything like it, straight over the crossroads it went, and the fruit and veg van screeching out the way, then it knocked down a wall and finished up in Mr Price's garden.'

'What, him that wins prizes with his chrysanths?'

'Won't be winning any prizes this year.' She laughed as she flushed the loo, then carried on the story by the sinks.

'Old Florrie Griffiths, she gets on her high horse— 'course it's her nephew drives the fruit and veg van— says it's a wonder no one was killed and she rings the police. I says to her, I says what do you want to go and do that for, that won't do any good, but she's ranting blue murder and then this Panda car turns up. Bloke on his own, wet behind the ears, uh-oh I thinks, and of course he gets out the car and he's doing his "What seems to be the problem, then?" and Florrie's going on at him about arresting the kids and while he's listening to her, young Wayne—you know Wayne, him with the red hair—he opens the door of the police car, lets off the handbrake, one good shove and that's off down the hill as well. You should have seen the look on the copper's face.'

'Wish I had seen it,' said her friend. 'Sounds better'n the telly.'

'You bet. Well, anyway, the copper radios in for help, takes an hour and a half for them to arrive, six squad cars screaming up, lights flashing, 'course by that time—'

The door slammed, shutting off the rest of the story.

She made that up, I thought. That can't be true. I peered out round the cubicle door. No one there. I caught sight of my face in the mirror. It looked strange. You may be scared witless, I told myself, but there's no need to look like it.

I hurried down the corridor, past some women who were standing talking. I kept my head down but felt them looking at me, felt their eyes hostile, alien.

By the exit a phone was ringing, on and on. No one answered it.

The bus had gone. I was going to follow it, back down towards the town, but then I saw a whole pack of dogs coming from that direction. The Alsatian was amongst them. I suppose it was the same Alsatian. They were trotting quite fast.

I turned the other way, up the hill. The kittens were miaowing. I had to find somewhere to let them out, but first I had to get away from the dogs. I was going in the one direction I didn't want to go, but I didn't have any alternative. Each time I passed a side road the dogs seemed to spread out, herding me on, up the hill.

It was hot, stifling. The sky was heavy and seemed to be fixed just above the rooftops. The street was dusty, strewn with litter and broken glass, the pavement spattered with the pale circles of chewed gum and piles of dog mess.

There was no one about, no one I could see, but I could feel the walls watching.

On I went, always up, with behind me, silent, the trotting dogs.

The hill got steeper. Then the houses stopped, ending beneath a patch of waste ground, stony, trampled bare in places. Where there was grass it was grey and tired, leaning into sprawling brambles. The top of the hill was covered in trees.

I turned towards the wood, up a dusty track. The dogs carried on along the street. Perhaps they had not really been herding me, but they seemed to glance up at me as they passed, checking, like sheepdogs that have brought the flock to where the farmer wants it.

The hill went on getting steeper and my legs heavier till breathing hurt and I was so tired I just wanted to lie down where I was and sleep. Only I was too scared to stop. I could feel sweat trickling down my front and the ground churred and whined with invisible insects. I stared downwards watching as each foot in turn wobbled upwards through the dust.

The kittens were still miaowing and had made another smell. If I'd had the energy I'd have told them to shut up or I'd make them walk and see how they liked that.

At last I reached the shade of the trees. I followed the track on up, looking for somewhere to rest. The ground was all over brambles. Then, almost at the top of the hill, I found a patch under a line of huge beech trees where there were no brambles, only last year's leaves and prickly beechmast. I dropped the sleeping-bag in the shelter of a stone wall, dropped down on top of it, and opened the rucksack. A nasty smell came out of it and five rather nasty kittens. I'd run out of tissues. The kittens slunk around, all ears and eyes, but kept stopping to wash. Sometimes they even washed each other. I tried not to think about it.

I closed my eyes and gave myself up to feeling miserable. I didn't know why I'd bothered to hide because I didn't care if I was set upon by barbarians or torn to pieces by their dogs.

I kept hearing Zack sneering: 'Sophie Marriott, you're a waste of space.'

Mum and Dad shouting at me.

And then I had thought I'd show them, they'd miss me when I was gone, then they'd be sorry, but they just went to work as usual with the answerphone bleeping its thirty seconds to take a message. I could imagine them, watching the news as they ate their tea, thinking how nice and quiet it was without me and Zack would have an extra helping.

No one wanted me. There was nowhere for me to go. Everywhere was hostile stares and people muttering, 'No room for you. Disgusting. Shouldn't be allowed.'

A kitten rubbed up against me. I pushed it away. They got me into this mess.

'Sophie Marriott, you're a waste of space.'

Then I started crying. I was vaguely aware of kittens climbing into my lap.

I cried till I was empty then stopped. I wiped my face on my sleeves and blew my nose on the sleeping-bag. The kittens looked at me anxiously and asked for dinner.

After I'd fed them I put the radio on for something else to think about. I was just in time for another news bulletin and more disasters. Someone murdered in Northern Ireland, a disgraced politician made to resign, thousands of refugees fleeing a country I'd never heard of. I couldn't remember afterwards if it was twenty thousand or two hundred thousand. Either way I couldn't imagine it. With my eyes closed I could visualize one: a child with round belly, matchstick legs, hopeless eyes, trudging through the dust.

The radio went back to playing records, with the DJ cracking jokes in between.

There was a tree stump sticking into my leg. I stood up to find a space to rearrange the sleeping-bag and it was then it occurred to me it was a strange place to build a wall, on top of a hill like that. I realized there was a ditch around the hill and that the wall, or what bits of it were still standing, ran around behind the ditch on a sort of bank. It must be the remains of a castle.

There was rubbish lying around, bits of metal, a saucepan with a hole in it, even an old dustbin. I wondered why people bothered to carry garbage to the top of a hill to throw it away. Then I noticed a tree with blue leaves. Quite amazing it was, bright blue. I was walking over for a closer look when my foot kicked against something, a paint spray. Ford Escort blue. Annoyed at having been taken in, I threw the can as hard as I could. It whacked into a bush. Out of the bush came a rat. It was huge, and glared at me malevolently before oozing away into a bank of nettles.

From the top of the wall I could see the town spread out like a map, see it packed on to the valley floor between lines of hills. I could write in the names of the two rivers and the canal (disused) that meet at the marshes running down to the sea. I could add a caption *Population* and give the number at the latest census (but

I've forgotten) and name the principal industries (but people in the town just do what they do anywhere).

Perhaps there were walls around the town once. At any rate there's a wide road running around the edge of the town, separating it from the Hill.

Standing there looking down reminded me of a song Zack sings sometimes, about a Spanish nobleman who lives in a castle dominating a plain, watching day and night for the enemies to come who will make him a hero. Only they never do come, though he grows old waiting.

I didn't want to be a hero, not any more. I just wanted to go home. And I wasn't Don Pedro. I was one of the enemies.

I couldn't see the dogs now, just a crow pecking at an empty crisp packet. The mood I was in, it looked like a spy, ready to report in if I moved. I decided to stay where I was until dark.

It was the first time I'd really thought of the night as being somewhere that I could hide, rather than somewhere other things lurked. Now the prospect of darkness falling seemed more like a comfortable blanket, something to even the odds a bit.

I had another try at the computer game and this time found out how to shoot the alien spacecraft. The machine warbled each time some enemies blew up. I reached level two and carried on dodging meteors and zapping aliens until the batteries faded out.

By then the sun was setting behind the hill, casting a long shadow over the town. Lights started to come on, seeming very far away, like stars in another galaxy whose shining had died before ever I saw it.

Not all stories have happy endings. Mine looked as though it was turning out to be the other sort.

CHAPTER TEN

A crash woke me, deafening, like the world split in half. I started up, screaming.

Then there was silence, almost, just the echoes of the crash dying away.

Then there were whispers, scratching just below hearing. Whispers, and a laugh.

I huddled small, shaking, praying that the darkness would cover me.

Another laugh. Then a voice, low, mocking, calling, 'Come out, come out, whoever you are.'

I went flatter, trying to sink into the earth.

'Hey, look!'

'What?'

'A cat.'

'Don't be daft, they don't come that small. It's a mouse.'

'There's some more here.'

'Mm, tasty! I'll take them back for my python.'

'No!' I shrieked.

There were two boys under the blue-leafed tree. One said to the other, 'Told you, didn't I? I said there was someone there.'

'Shame,' said the other. 'I thought it was a devil.'

'It might be a zombie. It doesn't say a lot.'

'Give me my kittens back,' I said.

'It's a witch. Feline familiars.'

'We'll feed her to the crocodile, and the cats to the python.'

'Stop teasing her, you two.'

I screamed again, because for a moment I thought the darkness spoke, but it was another boy, only he was black and his clothes were black and I hadn't seen him at all until then.

'It's all right,' he said, flicking on a torch. 'Those two are nutcases. That's Mart and that's Bart.' He shone the torch at each in turn. 'My name's Chuck.' He shone the torch on himself. He had dreadlocks and an ear-ring and was nursing a guitar.

'Chuck Berry, I assume?' I said, sarcastically.

''Sright.' He started to play a tune. Mart and Bart joined in, banging on the saucepan, the dustbin and the sheets of metal.

'Your cats are all over the place,' said Chuck. 'How many are there?'

'Five.'

'What are they called?' asked Bart.

'Parsley, that one's Thyme, Sage, Rose, and Mary.'

Mart blinked. 'Why on earth did you call them that?'

'I know,' said Chuck triumphantly. He struck a chord and sang, 'Are you going to Scarborough Fair?'

I joined in, and we sang a couple of verses, with percussion accompaniment.

'Neat,' said Mart.

'You haven't told us your name,' said Chuck.

104

'It's Sophie.'

Chuck shook his head. 'Won't do. Will it?' he said to the others.

They shook their heads too.

'What are you talking about?' I said. 'That's my name.'

'No, Sophie won't do. With a voice like yours you've got to have a proper name.'

'What do you mean, a voice like mine?'

'A brilliant voice.'

'Magic.'

'Wicked.'

'Do you know this one?'

It was another of Zack's songs, and then another, and the moon came up and the stars came out and we went on singing. The boys had a giant bottle of Coke, and we passed it around, and carried on singing. Owls joined in, and kittens ran in and out of the shadows.

'I think I shall call you Floyd,' said Chuck. 'Your voice would suit a Floyd.'

I thought about it. I quite liked the feel.

'We should have went,' said Mart. 'It's late.'

'What about Floyd?'

'She could live in the dustbin,' said Bart.

'And the cats in the saucepan,' said Mart.

'What *are* you doing here with all these cats?' asked Chuck.

I explained.

'I'll take you all home to Mum,' said Chuck. 'The cats can sort out the rats.'

'You've got rats? I saw one in the bushes.'

'Everyone has rats round here,' said Mart. 'There's more rats than people.'

'Once I was going for a pee,' said Bart, 'when this rat stuck its head out of the water, then turned round and went back down again.'

'You're making that up,' said Chuck.

'I'm not. I didn't dare sit on that loo for weeks, I tell you.'

Chuck strummed a while, then sang,
'Are you plagued with rats everywhere,
Parsley, Sage, Rosemary and Thyme,
Rats in the loos . . .'

'. . . and rats on the stair,' added Mart.

It took a while, but we all contributed, and eventually it was just about perfect, and we sang:

> *'Are you plagued with rats everywhere,*
> *Parsley, Sage, Rose, Mary, and Thyme,*
> *Rats in the rooms and rats on the stair*
> *Filthy, smelly, and covered with slime?*
> *What you need is one of our cats—*
> *Parsley, Sage, Rose, Mary, or Thyme—*
> *A pounce and a snap will finish the rats*
> *Then you'll find that life will be fine.'*

The music finished with a crash. The boys were laughing like drains.

I stood up. 'I think I'd better be going.' Even to myself I sounded stupid, as if I'd come to tea, not singing in the dark with boys I didn't know. The music had made me forget and now I didn't know how to get away.

'Go where?' said Chuck.

'Home.'

'What are you going to do with the cats?'

'Oh—I'll take them to a friend. I just thought of her.'

'You just made her up.' They were all coming closer, hemming me in. 'What's the matter?' said Chuck. 'You afraid of us?'

The moonlight glistened on the ring in his ear.

'No . . . no, it's just I must go.' I tried to edge away but backed into Mart's foot.

'Where do you live anyway?' said Bart.

'She lives in the town,' said Chuck. 'You can tell by the way she talks. And look at the way she stands. They all stand up straight down there, stick their noses in the air.' He took a few mincing steps. 'That's why they make their dogs wear nappies, so they can walk like this without stepping in anything nasty.'

'Their dogs don't wear nappies,' said Mart.

'Do too. Bunch of weirdos down there. They don't have gardens, only plastic grass and plastic flowers in plastic tubs. They eat plastic too, and—'

'You're off your head,' said Bart.

'Not me,' said Chuck. 'I'm the only one that's sane.' He pulled a hideous face. 'You're nuts, and Mart's nuts, only not half as screwy as people in the town.'

'I'm not going to listen to this,' I said. 'I'm going.' I pushed Mart out of the way and picked up the rucksack. It stank. I threw it, hard as I could, into a bush.

'Temper temper,' said Chuck. 'What are you going to carry the cats in now?'

The kittens were all in a heap on the sleeping-bag. I bundled them all inside and set off down the path.

The boys followed me, whistling.

'Yum, yum, here I come,' said Mart. 'Here I come, my python, with kitten for your dinner.'

'Let's feed them to the rats,' said Chuck. 'Feed *her* to the python.'

'You're disgusting,' I said.

'All a matter of taste,' said Chuck. 'You only like the kittens because they've got fur. If they were bald they'd be as ugly as Bart.'

'I saw a hedgehog without any prickles last night,' said Mart. 'Horrible it was.'

'You didn't.'

'I did. On telly.'

I'd seen the same programme—it seemed like years ago—and I was about to say so when I realized they'd started fighting and now was my chance to escape.

The path was quite clear in the moonlight, darker than the grass, but steeper than I'd thought. Before I could help myself I was bounding downwards with giant strides like a picture in a book I had once of a man with seven league boots on, the bundle of kittens clutched in my arms and each stride longer than the last, till I seemed to hang while the world streamed backwards, till I swear I was flying.

But the boys came bounding too and screeching and suddenly, as the ground started to whack against my feet as it levelled out a bit towards the road, an engine screamed and lights came blazing up the hill and I was hurtling towards them too fast to turn but someone grabbed me and pulled me aside.

The car shot past, up the grassy slope, the lights bouncing as it lurched over the bushes till finally the engine stalled.

'Idiots,' said Chuck, and I found I was clutching his arm.

Several people jumped out of the car. There was a lot of shouting and laughing, then a whoosh as the car caught fire.

'Head cases, they are,' said Chuck. 'Come on, let's beat it.' He gave me a push and we were running again.

I was so terrified I followed him without thinking and only stopped when I thought I'd burst. I leaned against a wall, panting, then I realized Mart and Bart had disappeared. 'Where have the others gone?' I said, when I could.

'Home. You don't want to hang about when that lot are around. Wayne's gang. Maniacs, they are.' There was the wail of a police siren, quite close. 'Come on,' said Chuck. 'I live over there.'

I hung back. No way was I going into his house. Perhaps I could get to the police car, perhaps they would help.

'Oh, come on,' said Chuck. He grabbed my wrist and pulled me over the street and up a flight of steps. I was still trying to pull away as Chuck unlocked his front door and pulled me into the house.

'That you, Michael?' called a female voice.

'No. Burglars,' he said, towing me into a living-room

where his parents sat in front of *News at Ten*, his father doing the crossword in the local paper and his mother with her feet up knitting. The armchairs were the same as the ones at home, only newer.

They didn't look as if they were infested with rats.

Chuck went through another door and came back cracking open a can while I still stood there gaping. 'This is Floyd,' he said. 'She's got cats. Go on, get them out.'

I opened up the sleeping-bag and extracted a heap of cross, frightened black fur. The kittens, pausing only to spit, vanished as one under the sofa.

Mrs Berry's feet shrank beneath her. 'I think,' she said, 'they'd better go in Poll's cage. Would you like some coffee, Floyd?'

Without waiting for an answer she disappeared into the kitchen.

Mr Berry removed a blanket from a large cage in the corner of the room and opened the door. A grey parrot stepped out, took off and landed on the curtain rail, where she bobbed up and down a few times, fixed me with a cold black eye and said, 'Morning.'

You can't stay formal while trying to catch five small kittens under a sofa. They decided it was a game, and put paws out to prod then hid behind castors and each time we eased the sofa up one way the kittens seemed to dematerialize and come out the other. We, and they, kept finding things that had rolled under the sofa and by the time Chuck and Mr Berry and I had finally gathered up five kittens, two corks, a cotton reel, and eleven pens

110

we were out of breath but laughing as if we'd known each other for years.

'It's all right, Mum, you can come out now,' called Chuck, and Mrs Berry peered out from the kitchen. Seeing five kittens safely shut up in the cage she came in carrying a tray of coffee and biscuits. I was starving.

Through a mouthful of dunked digestive I said, 'I'm sorry they frightened you.'

'I'm not frightened,' said Mrs Berry, putting her feet up again. 'Not so long as they don't move. Pretty little things. Really.'

'Have another biscuit,' said Mr Berry, poking a pen through the bars of the cage for Parsley to grab.

'Um . . . what are you going to do with them?' asked Mrs Berry.

'I don't know,' I confessed. 'I rescued them, you see, from drowning, but my parents wouldn't let me keep them and then they were going to the Cats' Home but then I found out that when the Home is full they sell the animals for research.'

'I don't think that's right,' said Mrs Berry, taken aback. 'They don't do that sort of thing. My neighbour, she had her cat from there, she says they're very good. Always manage to find homes somehow.'

I said: 'I'll kill him.'

There was a pause.

'Who?' said Chuck.

'Zack. My brother. He *told* me . . .'

'I think,' said Chuck, 'he was having you on.'

At that moment the telephone rang. Everyone jumped, but no one went to answer it, and I realized it was ringing from the curtain rail. After a bit the parrot stopped ringing and said, 'Hello?'

'That's why we cover her up,' said Chuck. 'Otherwise she rings all night.'

I asked if I could use the phone and they said, 'Sure,' and left me in the hall with it.

I dialled home.

Dad answered, first ring.

He shouted for a bit, then Mum came on and she shouted and then burst into tears and Dad said, 'Now look what you've done,' and it took a while before they calmed down enough to listen to me. I told them— Chuck had told me—I was at 23 Elgar Terrace, behind Purcell Parade, and then there was some more shouting when they realized I was on the Hill.

Anyway.

It didn't take long for them to arrive, and I borrowed the parrot cage, which Chuck promised to come and collect. I gave him my phone number and we're going to write songs together.

On the way home it turned out the reason the answerphone had been on when I rang was that everyone was out looking for me. Zack had owned up to telling me lies about the Cats' Home and animal research and was going to have to apologize. So that was all right.

It was very late by the time everyone got to bed, and

I was shattered. So tired I couldn't sleep, and I realized I was hungry.

I tiptoed downstairs—the house was dark and quiet—and had a bowl of Rice Krispies. Rug came and licked the bowl when I'd finished and then curled up on my lap. The kittens were sleeping in their cage, and I thought they'd be great pets for someone else, and stroked Rug. I'd known him for ever, and he's always there to meet me when I get home. He purred.

I'm going to save up my pocket money for my own guitar. By Christmas, if I persuade Mum to trade the gift tokens I always get from aunts and people, I'll have enough.

And I'm not going to be called Sophie any more. I'm Floyd, and I'm going to be famous.

Other books by Jay Ashton

Looking for Ilyriand
ISBN 0 19 271646 8

Six people, a goose, a dog, and a talking dragon go on a quest to find the fabled country of Ilyriand. Some of them are looking forward to the adventure; some aren't so sure. And Prothero, the dragon, moans that he doesn't really want to go at all, thank you very much.

The legends say that Ilyriand is the perfect land. But does it exist? And will they find it in time? This is a funny, exciting fantasy adventure, peopled with some wonderful characters.

'Not only is *Looking for Ilyriand* full of fantasy, humour, adventure, and a wonderful talking dragon, but it also carries a quiet 'green' message about how we need to take care of the world.'
What's On

'A marvellous long read.'
Junior Bookshelf

The Door from Nowhere

ISBN 0 19 271689 1

Dylan finds out by accident that really he's adopted—
and suddenly his parents aren't his parents any more. He
leaves home on the spur of the moment, determined to
track down his real mother. But things don't work out
quite as planned. Dylan ends up living rough in an old
cowshed in the Welsh countryside, haunted by his
feelings and by echoes and emotions from the past.
And not only from his own past: other people's stories,
too, explore the problems and the challenges of what it
is like to be an adopted child.

'A delightful story, full of vivid portraits and sharply
humorous descriptions of people and places. It deserves
to be read and savoured.'
Junior Bookshelf

'A well-written and gripping tale ... a very good read.'
School Librarian

Killing the Demons

ISBN 0 19 271708 1

Sam can't even walk any more, not since the accident. But she refuses to accept what this does to her, refuses to put up with people's attitudes when they try to make her into a non-person.

Sam may be in a wheelchair, but she is determined to do things her way, even if sometimes it makes her unpopular. And there is one way that she can forget all the problems. Playing her computer games, she can walk again—and run and fly—acting it out on the screen and in her imagination. But Sam can't escape like this for ever. Eventually she must begin to come to terms with her life and future in the real world.

'Those who read this book will surely remember Sam: a very human character with faults as well as virtues and never anybody's fool.'
Times Educational Supplement

'A challenging work of fiction which demonstrates the difficulty in achieving real quality in human relationships. A winner.'
Books for your Children